Oktoober 2005a
Kallis Isa ja Momma,
Küll teie õpetasite
mulle palju!
Tänu ja tänu)
Linda

The Inner Green

Exploring Home in the Columbia Mountains

K. Linda Kivi
and
Eileen Delehanty Pearkes

MAA PRESS, Nelson, B.C. 2005

Cover painting by Carol Wallace (cwall@netidea.com)
Other illustrations by K.Linda Kivi and Eileen Delehanty Pearkes
Book design by Angela Lockerbie (lockerbie@shaw.ca)

Printed in Canada at Hignell Book Printing on 100% post-consumer use, recycled paper.

Published in Canada by Maa Press
1-4925 Marello Rd.
Nelson, BC,
V1L 6X4, Canada
e-mail: maapress@netidea.com
website: community.netidea.com/maapress

Library and Archives Canada Cataloguing in Publication

Kivi, K. Linda, 1962-
    The inner green : exploring home in the Columbia Mountains / K. Linda Kivi and Eileen Delehanty Pearkes.

Includes bibliographical references.
ISBN 0-9685302-1-4 (bound).--ISBN 0-9685302-2-2 (pbk.)

1. Natural history--British Columbia--Columbia Mountains. I.
Pearkes, Eileen Delehanty, 1961- II. Title.

QH106.2.B7K58 2005   508.7116   C2005-904910-3

This is, I think
what holiness is:
the natural world,
where every moment is full

of the passion to keep moving.

Mary Oliver

Contents

Preface

A cool breeze slides down the side of the narrow valley, bringing with it the scent of high mountains. The breeze carries the weight of snowmelt, the perfume of alpine wildflower and a whiff of flowing streams. When it arrives on the valley floor, it ruffles the heart-shaped leaves of a mature cottonwood tree standing like an old soul beside a river. On steep slopes framing the path of water, the spires of cedar, hemlock, Douglas fir and various pines blanket a rough underpinning of rock. They smooth the mountain flanks into lush, blue-green splendour.

Not long after the wind skirls through the valley, clouds appear over the high horizon of peaks, filling the sky with cool air and the promise of moisture. Thunder claps, then lightning flashes. Raindrops begin to fall in icy darts. After a while, the rain settles into a soft downpour as the wind dies back. Moisture drips from the sheltering height of the conifers, soaking into the rich black soil that barely covers the bedrock beneath. Rain nourishes the fern, moss and abundant greenery that feeds all the other animals in turn. Rain patters against a river turned the colour of steel. Here, so far from the British Columbia coast, a rainforest flourishes, a place of dense, green growth, temperate climate and water bound by rock.

The Columbia Mountains jostle closely against each other in this unique Inland Temperate Rainforest just east of the vast Interior Plateau. Here, most of the precipitation falls as snow which accumulates in bedded layers through winter. Three major mountain ranges assemble along north-south lines, parting only briefly here and there to host narrow lakes or rivers. The mountains give birth to North America's fourth-largest river, the Columbia, a river that begins its path on the eastern flanks of the Purcell Range and then threads south through the Monashee and Selkirk ranges, gathering copious snowmelt and rainwater from the steep landscape as it goes. Verdant, scenic and challenging, the Columbia Mountains produce nearly half of the Columbia River's abundant water, and obscure nearly half of the sky in the process. Also known as the Kootenays and the Upper Columbia Basin, the region trades open spaces for the firmness of sheltering mountains.

We both arrived in the Columbia Mountains along separate paths, but eventually found each other through our common fascination with the region's natural history. These pages record our homecoming journey to this place, a journey that, as it turned out, had an inward spiral as well. The process of moving into ourselves as we learned more and more about our outer world surprised both of us, but in the end, has made our arrival more complete. Home is much more than a place. It is also a feeling, one inspired by a connection between the human heart and the landscape. A connection to place can draw each and every one of us toward the inner green, a heart-vision of the living, natural world.

We share with you here the sudden, wet valleys and complex peaks of the Columbia Mountain region. If you already know them, we hope this book will deepen your knowledge or open you to new perspectives. In our explorations, we try to value nature's metaphysical power and mystery as much as its physical properties. We try to engage all our senses, to draw on indigenous knowledge as well as scientific observation. We gratefully acknowledge the Sinixt, the First People of the heart of the Upper Columbia Basin. These indigenous people are a cultural model for relating to land not just as a physical place, but as something beyond that. They were the first to arrive here. Over several thousand years, they lived in the Place of Bull Trout, a traditional territory bound by the Monashee Mountains in the west and the Purcell Mountains in the east. Their stories, beliefs, practices and cultural traditions have informed and guided our efforts to come home. We also acknowledge the cultural traditions of their neighbours: the Ktunaxa (Kootenay) to the east, the Secwepemc (Shuswap) to the northwest, and the Okanagan to the west.

Ironically, if we have one hope for this book, it is that you will put it down. Go ahead, lay it on the table beside your favourite reading chair and move outside, wherever you live — be it in an urban centre, in a half-wild rural place or out in raw wilderness. There, you will find a landscape that will spark your curiosity, challenge you and help you encounter your own inner green. The best knowledge of a homeplace is out there, and yet the most fruitful path outward often leads in. To live here has taught us to meet each moment, much as a leaf flutters in a cool mountain breeze. To be at once as fluid and sharp as a glacier-fed stream, as open and secretive as a fern, as persistent and soft as falling snow.

K.Linda Kivi
Eileen Delehanty Pearkes
June, 2005

Homecoming

K. Linda

The first sensation was one of sweet warmth, not my own body warmth, generated and trapped by familiar blankets and mattresses, but rather an earthly flush permeating up from the forest floor and encompassing me. An instant later, I heard the murmur of water. Twigs and moss embossed the skin of my cheek. The prickle of dried needles felt like a caress. I opened my eyes. Silence filled the sloped spaces between the sun-speckled trunks of trees. In one beam of light, a patch of heart-shaped wild ginger leaves glowed emerald green.

I unfurled my body from the forest hollow where I had fallen asleep. Rusty shards of the rotten cedar log that had spooned my back clung to my clothes. As I picked them off, my body sang with aliveness, a sense of connectedness and openness. My mind was quiet and present. I was part of the sun-dappled forest, a piece of the day at hand, integral to both place and time. I was not a shard of flesh separate from the landscape but contiguous with it — I felt inside of place, or perhaps place had entered me. Whatever it was, the picture window that had separated me from everything around me — even from myself — had shattered.

I fell asleep on a warm July slope above Bird Creek in the Inland Temperate Rainforest of the Columbia Mountains. I woke up in the centre of my world. My nap had split my life in two. For 37 years, my life story had been a spiralling, earnest search — conscious and unconscious — for a place in which I would finally feel at home, in myself and on the Earth. The moment had arrived. The rightness of belonging filled me. I had no need to be elsewhere.

I arrived both in this world and in the Columbia Mountains as a refugee. Up until that moment, the act of leaving had described my life, defined my psyche. During World War II, my parents fled their homeplace in the boggy lowlands by the Baltic Sea. Though I was born much later, I emerged into a culture smarting from the expulsion from its ancestral, indigenous home.

My parents' loss formed my understanding of home as much as did their longing to return. In the Estonian school, Estonian camp, Estonian Girl Guides, Estonian folk dance of my Toronto childhood, we refugee children, born in the "Free World," were plunged into honouring a faraway place unfamiliar to us. Our mother tongue, with its long vowels and soft consonants, enunciated a different landscape, a different time. We sang the praises of "the cuckoo, the golden bird," and followed "Little Manni, tiny Anni / going to the forest berry-picking / little Minni, tiny Ninni / quickly, quickly after them." Their baskets laden with lingonberries, cranberries and cloudberries,

I followed their adventures into the boggy boreal forest where big-eared European squirrels and pipe-smoking hedgehogs played storybook characters.

In my family and culture, Estonia, or at least a collective memory of the land known as Estonia, was celebrated in certain acts, words and especially songs. We raised our community of voices at every gathering to sing of our homeland of "happiness and joy," all the while remembering to add a thanks to Canada for having taken us in. In these ways, I learned of the great love that binds indigenous people to the land they belong to, where time and place are one and inseparable. But what happens when you remove people from this indigenous context? Place is lost; time is fractured. Worshipping Estonia in some downtown Toronto hall rendered this profound connection into something abstracted, ungrounded.

As I grew to adulthood, I went through the motions required of Estonian refugee life with less and less conviction. My brother and I were frequently chastised to "speak Estonian!" at home. Canadian words for which there was no easy Estonian equivalent infiltrated our conversations. I wanted to break with the past and all of its messy limitations. What did this history have to do with me? Estonia was a place to which we could not even travel. Was I not Canadian? Free? Did I not have this vast land in which to choose a place to be whoever I wanted to be? Did fear not limit people? Was the quest for security not just another trap? Being Estonian seemed to mean being small and afraid. I wanted to be big, to walk as though the world belonged to me, as many North Americans do.

It was thus that I became a refugee myself, in flight from my history, my culture of origin, my own spirit. Like countless North Americans — the most mobile people on Earth — I ran away. I travelled extensively in Africa, Central America and Europe. I studied

15

Feminism and International Development, versed myself in women's issues worldwide, read international literature, listened to world music, protested injustice and ate global cuisine. In spite of my insistence that one who wanders freely has nothing to lose, some tickling desire for a homeplace persisted. In spite of my headlong rush to become a modern, North American urbanite with sophisticated and politically astute global tastes, the natural world continued to lay claim to me.

Every chance I got, I travelled north to Muskoka, to the cottage my father built. I took my friends there. During the winter, we skied through the maple bush, lit fires in the wood stove and played my childhood board games. In the warmer seasons, we spent long hours plunging into the still black lake and drifting around the islands in a canoe. With time, I increasingly made the trek north alone, to write and just be. I learned how to putter in the woods, counting spring's red trilliums, listening to the cry of the loons, fingering and pocketing stones. There, I encountered my painful internal chaos and a yearning I could not articulate.

Naturalist and writer Aldo Leopold suggested the question we should be asking ourselves is not Who am I, but Where am I? Engaging with this question, however, brought up deep fears.

Home, in my family, was synonymous with loss and unfulfilled longing. War and displacement have very long arms. They reach down through generation after generation. My parents' *conscious* lessons instructed their children not in how to love, but in what to fear and how to protect themselves. The only bond possible with land was one of mythic proportions with a country my brother and I had never been to and had little hope, we all thought, of ever visiting in our lifetimes.

In spite of my parents' fears and modern, upwardly mobile hopes for my brother and me, my father, peasant that he is, could not conceal his reverence for the Earth. After supper, as long as evening light allowed, my father would slip on his worn shoes and walk slowly to the back of our yard where he spoke with cucumbers, caressed feathery carrot tops, built strawberry pyramids and watered a grape vine for whose products my mother failed to find a use. I watched him in his garden from my bedroom window. It was not a world he shared with us, but I witnessed it, witnessed the quietude this contact with the Earth brought him after his days among the jangling machinery of a carpentry shop. Every weekend possible, we braved northbound traffic to cottage country, and sighed a collective, familial relief when we smelled the potent, woodsy scent of our country home.

Eventually, both my brother and I found our way to the woods, in our respective parts of this continent, not squatting as city dwellers transposed or as foreigners in a fort, but as inhabitants of forest.

One June, during a conference jaunt to Vancouver and Calgary, a co-worker and I rented a car and drove between the two cities instead of flying. Halfway through the trip, we descended down into the Columbia River valley at Castlegar, B.C.. We crossed the high bridge over the brooding Columbia and traversed the valley. On the far side, we crossed the smaller, clearer Kootenay River and drove into a fold of the hills at Brilliant. The mountains took me in. There, below Verigin's Tomb, the burial place of the first Doukhobor leader in Canada, the narrow valley opened up, and the forested slopes encompassed me. It was a welcome that touched me deeply. Even now, I ponder why that place spoke to my yearning for home. Was it the forest, tall and dense with an incredible variety of trees? Was it the cool, clear lakes? Was it the mountains that enfolded me, like a mother's arms?

When I returned to Ontario, the place stayed with me, but what enabled me to make the move was a surprising turn of events on another continent. In 1989, when Perestroika rusted a hole into the

17

The Inner Green

Iron Curtain, I travelled "back home" to Estonia. In a peat bog where the pine-filtered light revealed the glowing jewels of lingonberries, cranberries and the occasional slippery mushroom, I uncovered the passageway home. It was as if, lying in foot-deep spongy moss, my two hands plucking berries in an ancient, ritualistic way, my ancestors bestowed upon me my inheritance of a home-dweller: the ability to love the land. Exuberant, I did not want to leave when my cousin came by with her berry-burdened basket to take me home. The evening sun slanted through the forest as I dawdled after her. I fell so far behind that I decided to take a short cut through the ditch. From the bridge, my cousin called out to me, but it was too late. I had stepped into what had seemed like the solid ground of the ditch and sunk in up to my hip. I was stuck and sinking in the cool muck. My cousin had to heave and pull for many minutes before my leg emerged, the green slime closing behind it with one great sucking sound. Puzzled, she did not say what she was thinking: even an Estonian child would know not to step there. Thus came the first lesson of a dweller in place: living in place requires as much knowledge as love. Without both, we are either babes in the woods, or destroyers.

The next spring, I packed my bags, filled my truck and drove myself into the folds of the Columbia Mountains. I came to lay down my roots. I understood how new I was, as ready for schooling as I had been when I entered kindergarten and, as in kindergarten, needing to learn a whole new language to make sense of the world. In my conscious mind, I was coming to an artsy area (the Nelson area), with a large socially alternative community (including a queer community), where acreages were cheap, the forests abundant and the growing season was long enough to grow tomatoes. Nineteen eighty-nine was, coincidentally, the same year the Sinixt reclaimed responsibility for their homeplace in these valleys of abundant water. Against many

18

odds, they had refused to let their kinship with this land be extinguished. Their persistence continues to inspire me not to flee but to face adversity and disruption with aplomb. The geographic solution that truly succeeds in creating deep and persistent connections with Earth is to stay put, the more generations the better.

I have no idea how long I slept that day in my warm hollow on the slopes above Bird Creek or how many minutes I sat breathing the liquid air before I gathered my pack and continued downstream. What remains clear was the sharp beauty of every plant I passed, every rock I stepped upon, every fallen tree I scrambled along, every squirrel who scolded, every bird who slipped quietly past me through the shadows. Every living and sedentary Earth part became individual and alive. As did I. From that moment, I became more than reliant on the natural world; I became part of it.

Eileen

A friend of mine believes that it is possible for us to carry two home places in our hearts: the natural landscape of our childhoods and a second landscape, one that matches our individual preference and destiny. For the first twenty years of my life, I lived in the oak savannah of coastal California. I was surrounded by arid light that could be both golden and white hot. Hills rolled gently and spaciously. Grassland crackled in the heat. Infrequent trees dotted the landscape, spreading their limbs wider than they were tall. The sky shared its space with only one mountain in my childhood, a rather modest peak called Mt. Diablo. Otherwise, vistas were open, expansive and bright. Nothing about my childhood environment prepared me for my attachment to the steep, wet and shadowed Columbia Mountains. Nothing, except for the love of the natural world that I witnessed in my grandfather and mother on my grandfather's ranch in central California. Their lessons were universal. I brought them with me to make them my own in this place.

I recall sitting in the ranch house on a hot summer day more than 30 years ago. I was a small child. The house, with a wide veranda, stucco walls and bare linoleum, was a cool retreat from the searing midday heat. I was filling in a new colouring book with stubs of crayon saved by my grandmother. My mother was reading in a chair, the glossy pages of her magazine snapping efficiently as she turned them. My grandfather sat at the large kitchen table that adjoined the living room. The clock ticked on the mantelpiece. In the cool quiet, my grandfather had begun to doze, his eyelids wavering, his chin tilting toward his once muscular chest.

"What's that?" he said suddenly, as if he had never been asleep. Dishes began to rattle. "Earthquake, Mary," he said to my mother. I did not look up. The room began to tilt and move. Books on the shelf above the piano began to wiggle. The sky on my page in the colouring book had begun to fill out so beautifully, so evenly and so blue. I didn't want to leave it. As the rumbling grew more intense, my grandfather made a decision. "Let's get out of here," he said urgently.

"Eileen," my mother said, "Eileen, we need to get outside!"

The rumbling continued to strengthen. I had lived through several small tremors by that time in my childhood. All earthquakes seem to be more or less the same size at first. The longer the quaking goes on, the stronger the tremor becomes. Earthquakes can last a few seconds, or several minutes. By this time, more than a minute had passed. I had the crayon at just the right angle for the colour to be applied smoothly. Now the page had begun a slow dance beneath my fingers.

"Eileen!"

My mother yanked me to my feet and pushed me, crayon in hand, out the front door. As I ran past the wire fence enclosing the yard of the ranch house, cracks formed before my eyes in the cement pathway. Fear finally overtook me. I stumbled over the cracks. My mother pushed me through the squeaking metal gate and across the dirt road, to open pasture where dark smudges of oak trees gathered along a coulee at its fringe. We stood in the open: my grandfather, my mother and I, while the Earth thundered beneath our feet and the dust rose around us. I don't remember where my older brother and sister or my little sister were. My grandmother must have been there, too, but I don't remember her standing with us. I remember only my grandfather, my mother and me.

My grandfather knew from experience that the safest place during an earthquake was in the open, far from any buildings. I did begin to feel safe, oddly enough, standing in the open with cattle nearby and a sky bleached by heat. Gradually, the Earth began to settle into stillness again. We waited. My grandfather and mother wondered to each other about aftershocks. It had been what Californians refer to as "a big one." My grandfather said he thought it was over. We walked carefully back across the road, through the gate and down the pathway. My grandfather assessed the cracked sidewalk. My mother stooped with him, measuring.

Nearly every summer, our family journeyed a four-hour drive south from our San Francisco Bay Area home to spend a week or more in the place where my mother grew up, a ranch in central California. An hour inland from the ocean, it was near the famous San Andreas fault-line and experienced regular earthquakes: small tremblings, whispers of movement or occasionally, like during that summer, big ones. I learned a harsh lesson about the natural world that day when the concrete cracked, and gentler lessons, in smaller ways, during all my summer visits with my mother, on the land she and her family knew very well.

My grandfather had handed the active work of the ranch over to my uncle by the time I was old enough to remember visiting them. But he was drawn onto his land daily all the same. He owned several thousand acres. He had pieced this whole together from many separate smaller ranches acquired through sweat and hard work over several decades. Though he no longer ran the show, he liked to keep his hand in. He would create reasons to go out, whistling sharply for his dog Pup, who leapt eagerly into the back of the pickup. Once, I rode with him to check out a fence that was down. On this ride, I recall, my grandfather slowing the truck at one point as we drove along a pasture road and stabbing his finger toward the windshield.

"Quail!" he said.

I tried to see the birds, but by the time my eyes focused on their feathers, I saw only the tips of a few tails disappearing into the blond safety of wild grass. Without my grandfather's guidance, I would have missed them altogether. I could sense a respect for those who knew how to move quickly to avoid danger, whose delicate feathers could elude the solid metal of a hunting rifle.

On another drive, I was flung off the pick-up seat when he braked hard and abruptly. My bare legs peeled from the vinyl and my forearms braced against the dash. Beside me, my grandfather's usually harsh and scowling face had softened. There, in a draw shaded by manzanita scrub and mature oak, I saw a deer and her fawn poised to move. The mother's chest nudged against the delicate fawn. She was alert to potential danger. I could feel my grandfather's obvious affection for these delicate animals move across the seat to settle beside me. I felt reassured somehow, that an avid hunter could have also respected and admired the animals he stalked in appropriate seasons. My grandfather had always intimidated me. I grew less afraid of him after that.

He seemed to take stock of all the creatures on his land, from the black and white clacking of a whisky jack perched on a weathered fence post, to the almost indiscernible flash of a summer-brown feather as it disappeared into the brush. His father had been a store-keeper. His brother became a dentist. For some reason, he was drawn into the landscape. He may have sensed in the Earth a force that sur-passed his own strong personality and physical strength. My mother, who was born on the ranch early in the Great Depression and raised there until young adulthood, probably learned acute observation from her father. She captured butterflies and bugs as a child and went on to study botany at university. Several years ago, when she fell ill with Alzheimer's disease, I found an old cigar box way at the back of a hallway cupboard in our family home. I opened it and discovered one of her carefully arranged, precisely labelled collections of butter-flies, painted with the same vivid colours that had once announced their presence in the grass. My mother pinned them to the cardboard long ago. She looked up all their Latin names, identifying through observation the colouring and wing shape that made each one unique. She captured them for science, but also for placement.

My mother loved to break the stems and leaves of plants to sniff them and be reminded of what they were. "Bay laurel," she would reply when I brought her a leaf to be identified and she had broken it in two. Or, "live oak," fingering the glossy, dark-green smoothness. Or, "oat grass," popping a tiny grain from the husk into her mouth and giving it a chew. If she didn't know the name of a plant when we were somewhere unfamiliar, she would look it up later in her black and white illustrated botany texts. When the family drove along back roads, during camping trips, she inevitably would ask my father to pull over, so that she could gather some large sugar pine cones she had spotted, or an array of blooming branches that interested her.

Both my mother and grandfather called me to attention, pushed me out the door to safety. It seems contradictory, that safety would be found outdoors rather than indoors. I have often reflected on the fact that I was safest outside on the day the earthquake shook my world. Such a notion is contrary to the fortress mentality of colonials who settled the Canadian wilderness. Outdoors, cold and danger lurks. Indoors, warmth and safety reign. Ironically, only human-constructed shelter could create danger in an open, oak savannah poised on an ancient fault line. My childhood experiences in the dry, gently rolling hills taught me not to fear nature, but to worship it.

Attempts to develop a relationship with many landscapes followed in the first decade of my adult life, as I moved from California to France, back to California, to New England and finally to coastal B.C. Though I had returned to the ranch house that day, a part of my spirit had remained outside. A wild morsel of my being had taken refuge in the filigree of oak. From then on, it followed me wherever I went. It was always outside, clinging to rhythms of the Earth. Over the years, it whispered two questions, over and over: *Do you know where you are? Do you know who you are?* My wanderings were all extensions of that first push out the door during the earthquake. As I changed jobs, married, changed jobs again and gave birth to children, that wild bit of myself hovered overhead at the edge of the stars, swam in the flash of a wave, or stuck itself to a damp scarlet leaf lying on the ground.

When I entered the valleys of the Columbia Mountains, I could feel that wild morsel's voice rise, urging me to stay. But why so very far from my childhood landscape, in a place that did not even remotely resemble it, had I finally arrived home? It has taken me years to understand what the wild part of me already knew: that the mountains towering around me offer an example that no other place has yet suggested. A source of strength and solidity, an immovability and drama. They attach firmly to the ground, yet also touch the sky. In their placement, they are at once of the Earth and above it, capable of reaching great heights. I see a mountain out every window of my house. I pass mountains on either side when I enter or leave the narrow valley where I live. I find mountains in all directions when I boat on Kootenay Lake. I watch them ripple into the distance for kilometres when I climb out of the valley to a high ridge. They insist their presence in this place, calling me to ground myself and yet also to raise my spirit high. I experienced my earliest feelings of love for this region on the warm, pebbled beaches of Kootenay Lake, where the massive shoulders of the mountains held me and offered their strength, showing me the sky and the Earth at the same time.

It has occurred to me that my lack of lineage in this land calls into question my loyalty to any place, though it sharpens my curiosity and humbles my knowledge. Don't I belong in California, the landscape of my birth and childhood? I could have easily taught my children how to sled, not on drifts of snow, but the way a California child does, down grass hillsides on flattened appliance boxes in the searing heat of summer. I could have snapped a leaf in two and told them its name. I could have shown them how to crack open and then grind the meat of acorn, how to chase and then capture a tendril of fog in their hand. I could have driven them down the rutted tracks of my grandfather's ranch, picked artichokes from the garden for them to eat and showed them the olive groves peppered with oily fruit. I could have stayed in the arid California hills. Instead, I have come here to learn alongside my children, in a landscape that casts perplexing shadows. I have travelled far in order to understand what it means to be local. Now, I fumble and listen. I adapt and experience. I have learned that one can fall in love with landscape the same way one falls in love with a perfect stranger or an old, familiar friend.

Welcome home, I have said to myself many times in the past few years. I know that the journey has ended, here in the cool, complex Upper Columbia River watershed. Such an unlikely home for the girl who felt the searing openness of an oak savanna, who still loves how her childhood landscape feels, who understands it in her bones. But then I look up toward the rickrack pattern of peaks that shrink the sky in the place where I now live. I feel the geography of cleaved rock and rushing water hold me tightly, in the valley around the Kootenay River. I utter a simple prayer of thanksgiving that I have arrived, to learn what this place has to teach.

Thank you mountains, for showing me the way.

The Weight of a Name

K.Linda

...I hold me down
with rocks I put in my pockets
...Weighty little chunks
of my country
hold me to it
ever more nearly

Ursula K. LeGuin

It is a breathtaking and completely unexpected sight. As we careen around a corner on the rough backcountry road, a white tower appears from between the dark, tree-splattered slopes we are travelling through.

My partner, Martin, pulls the truck to a halt. We gaze up the valley at the formation that rises, smooth and pale, from behind the surrounding peaks. It gleams in the midday sun against the backdrop of the blue sky. I have been sick for 10 days and still, weakly, recovering, I wonder if I'm hallucinating. I roll down the window and survey the vegetation at the roadside. No, everything is as it should be, thick stalks of cow parsnip mingling with false Solomon's seal, horsetail and the rest of the usual cast of characters. I look back up. The ivory mountain is still there.

Clearly, it can't be a glacier. They nestle in concave depressions, not dome out, like an enormous thumb, reaching toward the sky. There is only one thing it could be: rock. Martin ignites the engine and we continue our journey up. The pale monolith slips in and out of view as we round corners, negotiate treacherous creek crossings where the road has washed away with the spring freshet and switchback up the steep slope. The road keeps rising, as the friends we were meeting said it would, rising up until we pass through a notch and pop into a pass almost at the tree line.

The mountain towers in front of us. To the left of it rises another pillar of ivory rock. To the right, three more peaks thumb the sky. Each is as bare and treeless as the next. Martin notes that they are arranged in a north-south line, like an upturned seam of rock. On either side of this seam, the neighbouring peaks are contrastingly dark, jagged, crumbly and pocked with plants and trees almost to their summits. A quick look at the topographic map suggests that the pale seam of rock continues; if we were to climb one of these peaks, we would undoubtedly see a series of similar peaks. Nobody's enthusiasm could have prepared me for the sight of the Badshots.

I can barely take my eyes off the mountains. Martin drives up the eroding road out of the pass to survey the area for camping spots. I crane my neck not wanting, not able, to look at anything else. My only input is that he choose a site with a good view. It isn't until I unfold the lawn chair I brought along to convalesce in, and plunk myself down to behold the sight, that I begin to notice the rest of the landscape. In the backdrop, far beyond the deep Duncan River valley that separates the Badshots in the Selkirk Range from the next one to the east, are the ice-fields and peaks of Bugaboo Provincial Park in the Purcell Range. Around and beyond them, the mountaintops extend as far as the eye can see. Slumped in my chair, I feel appropriately weak and small and I am only too happy to let Martin unload the truck and set up camp on his own. This is usually not the case. I am made of solid stuff.

Rock has always had special meaning for me. My name, Kivi, means rock in my mother tongue, Estonian. I am actually named after a specific rock in Estonia, one that juts out of the lake that supplies drinking water for the denizens of the capital city. The rock is called "Linda Kivi" after Linda, the mother of Estonia's epic hero Kalevipoeg who carried it to this location and cried a lake of tears after her husband died. I do not take rock lightly.

At the same time, faced with the lithic spectacle in front of me, I realize how little I know about the substance whose name I bear. For the first time, I comprehend the fascination that geology holds. It is as though this unusual place had pulled me across the invisible line that divides those who peer deep into rock and its origins from those who merely see it. These two worlds are so disparate that to switch camps is akin to being a trash metal head who turns into an opera aficionado overnight. The transformation is internal and profound.

In my daily life, rock has been all too easy to ignore. Though stones spring eternally from our garden soil at home, and I am forever moving them around, building walls and pathways, my interest in them has always been limited to how they look and feel. The lushness of what is above ground, what is growing, usually commands my intellectual curiosity. In our places of human convergence and commerce, we move through a world full of the present moment. The past, especially the distant past, slips effortlessly to the back of our minds. Who remembers the story of rock, and what is the story of this rock?

The summer before, I had visited Lesley Anderton, the geology instructor at the local Selkirk College, in an attempt to crack open the story of the Columbia Mountains. With her greying head and solid body, Lesley resembles a fine, flecked chunk of granite. After over 30 years of teaching geology as well as giving talks, writing papers and being interviewed for articles, Lesley has become the resident authority on local geology. Amidst her stories about the Purcells, the Selkirks and the Monashees — the three chains that make up the Columbias — she told me something about the Badshot Range. But what was it? My 'flu-weary brain can't quite grasp it. She had a term for this place. She had a story.

Our friends arrive at dusk. I tear myself away from my viewpoint as darkness descends to join the evening's conversation and activity. With John and Coby, we share the camaraderie of those who choose to travel in the mountains together. Though we see little of each other in our daily, valley-bottom lives, our paths have often converged in the alpine of this continent and others. As Martin, Coby and John lean over a map on the tailgate, illuminating it with their headlamp beams, they plan the next day. Knowing I lack the strength for a vigorous day of climbing and scrambling, I lean back and let their familiar banter wash over me. They discuss their options, deciphering elevations and landforms from the contour lines on the paper. In the end, they decide to head off next morning through another pass, into a drainage that is said to be pristine. Even caribou have been seen there.

They set off after breakfast. As they disappear over a rise, I pull out my plant guide and, after a brief sit in the lawn chair, decide to putter close to camp. At first, I poke among the dense clumps of pink and white mountain heather around the camp, my hat brim pulled forward to shade my face. Although I scan the ground for alpine blossoms, it is rock above that keeps drawing my eye, tempting me to attempt a climb up the steep slope. I feel my energy returning, almost as if I am drawing it directly from the strength of the miraculous landscape. Even so, I debate the merits of wandering off. The sun is already hot and high in the blue August sky. What if I get into a tricky situation? My companions won't be back until late. I should rest.

As the sun starts tipping toward the west, I can't resist. Ten days of bed and hammock are enough! The tower lures me up and up, and I feel as though I am at its mercy. Mercy! How often do we allow ourselves to realize that we *are* at the mercy of the place where we live? Rock *is* the foundation of this mountain ecosystem. It precedes all the rest, and defines so much of what is to follow. Where it crops up out of the Earth's skin, ancient history is laid bare. Rock is where home begins for everyone and everything that dwells here. There is no older resident of the Columbia Mountains. Underground, to soil and to rock, is where the past goes. Sooner or later, in one way or another, we join it. Physically, our bodily minerals — our rock — return to the Earth. Our lives become, eventually, part of the past that rock represents.

Is this why people seek out mountains?

A gust of wind tears at my hat as I stop to catch my breath. I look back down on the treed campsite and then up at the edge of the white mountain above me. I'm halfway there. Already the soil has thinned so that only the hardiest of grasses and flowers can cling to the lichen-encrusted bedrock. Here and there, the rock protrudes. I pull out my water bottle and sit to drink. Like many people, I experience a sensation of profound well-being, akin to spiritual exaltation, in the alpine. The daily-ness of life is far away. While our human smallness in the face of such massive, old geological beings unnerves some people, I am among those who take great comfort from seeing themselves in the context of a great, still-unfolding story.

Lime. Lesley's voice whispers to me. *A lime* _____. What was it she called this rock feature? The half-remembered thought pesters me as I scan the slopes above and below me. Perhaps I will recall if I start at the beginning and remember what I've learned about this great geological tale.

Richard and Sydney Cannings' *British Columbia: A Natural History* contains a wonderful map entitled "Terranes" that recently enlightened me. Somewhere right under where I am sitting — sweating in the hot sun — is where the edges of the ancestral continent of North America and new terranes join. Before there was a British Columbia, the low shore of the ancestral continent was east of where the Rocky Mountains are today. That means this land and the Rockies to the east would have been under water.

About a billion years ago, Ancestral North America began to move, splitting apart the ancient land mass known as Rodinia. As the space between the newly formed continents stretched, water rushed to fill the divide. Then, there was a long calm. All that is now western North America was under a churning sea. On the ancestral continent, the land stretched far, rippled not unlike the sea. Every year, sediments from the land washed into the sea, laying themselves down, layer after layer until they were kilometres thick. Eventually, simple organisms began to form in the shallow waters. Time passed. Fern-like trees sprouted. All the while, the skeletons of these early life forms laid themselves down. Slowly the continental shelf formed.

About 170 million years ago, mountain building began. If I could have floated in this very spot for long enough, this land would have grown and shifted and folded under and around me, bucking me about like a bronco. I could have watched burning land sail over the water and crash into the shore, causing the thick rock beds to groan and rise. I would have seen supergroups metamorphose, subducting, releasing magma through thrust and block faults, plutons rising up through volcanic arc island terranes. The molten soup of geology terms washes over me and my head begins to spin. Landscape and rock are so concrete; it seems ironic that the language of their description is so abstract, so hard to grasp.

I will myself to my feet and continue climbing the slope, heading toward the closest clump of stunted alpine fir to get a bit of shade. As I climb, however, I am unable to resist picking up rocks and examining them. On a rising hump of bedrock just below the trees, I come across a protrusion of rock that resembles a series of miniature goblin dwellings. Layered tunnels lace the crystalline rock, sandwiched between sheets of dark, glistening grey. Clumps of lichen and moss cling to the rough surfaces. Each rock I stoop to gather is a different, magical universe. The mystery of the tall peaks above me is momentarily forgotten as I rummage through the gnome and goblin worlds. They are so contorted they seem as though they were the result of some terrible pressures.

As the volcanic island arc and ocean floor terranes collided with our ancestral continent, the machinery of tectonic plates set to crumpling, contorting, warping, thrusting, jolting, twisting, heating, ramming, plunging, rising, recoiling, reverberating, slipping, lurching, creeping, seeping, heating, deranging, oozing, percolating, swilling, rippling, quivering, writhing, quavering, squirting, telescoping, folding, reforming, sliding. I realize the trick is not to speed it up in my mind but to slow it down. Not to think of a massive car crash. All this occurred over a period of 100 million years, slowing down around 60 million years ago but continuing still.

Geologist Chris Yorath wrote about this process that:

"Of all the places in the Cordillera, it seems that the rocks of the Kootenay Arc have suffered the greatest agony. During the Paleozoic Era the rocks were folded, then later broken by thrust faults. Then, came the collision ... when everything was heated up, metamorphosed and folded again. Some 60 million years later they were intruded by huge masses of molten granite. Then, as if that wasn't enough ... the entire arc was detached from its basement and thrust eastward to its present position. Finally, as a sort of last kick at the cat, the rocks of the arc were stretched, broken up ... and squirted with hot magma again. The result of all this is an unbelievable mess to unravel."

But how to make any sense of it? I go cross-eyed thinking of these individual rocks in terms of millions of years of geological history. My goblin rocks have suddenly become more than inanimate, pretty curiosities; they have become pieces of the globe that have travelled far, seen a lot and changed much. When I hold them, I indeed hold the past in my hands. After a thorough examination of a few dozen rocks, I gather two sandwich-sized gnome villages and slump into the shade. These rocks will join the others that collect on my windowsills. I lie back onto the lumpy, prickly ground and close my eyes.

Rocks have needed no geological explanation to delight me. When I've gathered stones, I've hunted for interesting shapes, colours, textures. Common rocks, odd rocks, it was all the same to me. "I like rock," I would say when people commented on my collections. My name means rock, as if to imply there's something to a name. When I visit certain friends, I take them a rock or two. Their rocks, like my twisted gnome villages, migrate to windowsills, mantelpieces, gardens.

It's hard to find a human being who doesn't admire an odd rock or two. We transform them into metal, or maintain them as gems. We pay money for them and string them about our bodies. Our modern lines of communication, our modern methods of living rely on the minerals found in rock: copper for our pipes and wires, iron for our nails, even glass for our bottles and windows. Human beings spend much time and energy digging rock from the ground, often at great cost to the land and the people of mining areas. My father worked as a stone mason when he first came to North America. I, too, have built stone walls, learned to fit shapes together and set one rock next to another. Rare are those of us who do not touch rock daily, relate to it in some way. But, for the most part, we have been content to leave our heads in the proverbial rock fragments known as sand when it comes to reading its embedded history, understanding how it arrived to be where it is, as it is. But collecting rocks without understanding their stories is like listening to songs in languages we don't understand; the music is universal, but the meaning embedded in the lyrics is lost on us.

After a good rest, I continue uphill. The steep scramble leaves me puffing but there's no turning back now. I reach the narrow ridge that connects the land of the pass to the white monolith in front of me. I pick my way across until dark boulders turn to pale at the base of the magnificent mountain. Up close, I see that a few plants dot the lower reaches where crevices have allowed some soil to pool. I climb up to sit among the fragmented ivory chunks. Unlike the other rock lower down, this rock breaks off in long narrow pieces with smooth planes,

35

some over a metre long. Up close, I see that it's not pure white but shades of cream and yellow, with the occasional dark line running through it. When Lesley's term comes to me, I jump up and say it out loud. "Lime dyke! Lime dyke!"

The feature was named by early prospectors; dyke is an old Scottish word meaning wall or ditch. Though dyke is used by geologists only for igneous intrusions, the old prospectors' name for the Badshot feature has stuck. Unlike an igneous dyke, this massive wall of limestone is a bit of the continental shelf that formed over millions of years as skeleton after skeleton of ancient ocean creatures crumbled to the sea floor. Somehow, it got wedged between other layers of rock and turned on its side. Somehow, it survived the great crushing and metamorphosing impact on the Lardeau Group and maintained its sedimentary integrity. High on my mountain perch, far from any ocean, and 2600 metres above sea level, I caress the smooth face of a substance made from generations of living ocean creatures, in a time eons before human beings evolved. What was once a teeming mass of simple organisms has transformed into pillars of imposing rock rising out of a carpet of forested valley. But why is it here, so far from the other bits of continental shelf that make up mountains, like the Rockies, to the east?

As part of the Lardeau Group, one of the great geological unknowns of the area, the many layers of rocks in this area are cut across by the fault that created Kootenay Lake and extend southwest to Nelway on the U.S.–Canada border. The rocks are only slightly older than those of the Rocky Mountains but are much more metamorphosed. Though there are several theories, geologists may never agree whether it is local rock, meaning something that got heaved up off the continental shelf of Ancestral North America during mountain-building, or a piece of one of those foreign terranes that broke off during the collision.

In any case, now that I recall its name, I remember Lesley telling me that the edges of this formation are rich with minerals. I peer down the other side of the narrow ridge as I make my way back across and notice, for the first time, the eroded slope below that is intersected by what look like roads. Could this have been one of the mine sites? A growl from my stomach keeps me from the long detour it would take to get a closer look. Gorp and my lawn chair await me at our camp.

It is almost dark by the time my friends return to camp, full of tales of their day. We cook ourselves a supper of noodles and sauce and they fill me in on their adventures. In the next watershed over, they discovered the line of limestone continuing, forming a spectacular pale cliff that dropped into an alpine lake. Though they saw no caribou, they are elated with their day. After supper, Martin reaches into his pocket and deposits a rock in my hand. I turn on my headlamp to get a better look at the heavy lump, which is about the size of a plum with a glistening, multi-faceted, dark-grey surface. I measure its heft in my palm. "Galena?"

"Perhaps. I found it on the carved-up slope just the other side of this ridge." He points in the direction of the disturbed slope I had seen from the ridge. Galena is the mineral that was sought after in the Columbia Mountains. It is mined for its lead content and its associated zinc and silver deposits. Usually, galena is associated with the areas where granite and the old volcanic rock meet. Granite is formed when some of the Earth's magma rises up into the crust and cools very slowly. When granite cools, mineral fluids form and, because of pressure, seek a way out. The nearby "country rock," which is mostly volcanic in origin in these parts, is often cracked and fissured from its rough ride, and the mineral liquid races through its dark channels until it cools. There it crystallizes into a range of minerals.

The Inner Green

Closest to a granite intrusion, you get gold, and farther away, you get silver, zinc, copper, lead. At the edges of the granitic intrusions, especially where the swirling green bands that represent volcanic formations meet granite, are found the mining centres of the Columbias: Rossland, the Sandon area, the Bonningtons southwest of Nelson, Riondel on Kootenay Lake. But why are there mines here? Up against the lime dyke? How did this rich deposit come to be? I resolve to ask Lesley about the Badshots as soon as I get home. In the meantime, sleep beckons.

We wake up the next morning to a socked-in alpine. The mountains have disappeared into the mist and fog. A cold drizzle pinches my skin when I jump outside to pee, and though I know I'm playing with fate by spending time in this weather so soon after a prolonged illness, I cannot resist the lure of the mountain. Coby and John pack up to leave as Martin and I cross the pass and head in the direction of the first of the pale mountains we spotted. We follow a road that traverses the slope, passing by the most incredible colour array of paintbrush plants I have ever seen. Their upper leaves glow creamy white to salmon to magenta to crimson in the mist. The road continues up and up, even past the collapsing remains of an ore tramline and other buildings. Soon, the flattened roadbed is composed of nothing but the salt and pepper of broken rock as it skirts a glacier a few hundred metres wide. We stare upward in disbelief as we see that the road actually rises above the other side of the icefield.

To me, this road seems like the ultimate disrespect of mountain, sacrilege even. But mining is also one of the stories of this rock, of these mountains. Seeking fortune, the "49ers" of the 1849 California gold rush began to arrive in the Columbia Mountains in the 1860s, to pan for gold and prospect. They started at 49 Creek just west of Nelson and spread out, starting a mining boom that was the talk of the

38

day even in London, England. This boom precipitated the establishment of towns such as Nelson, Rossland, Trail, Sandon, Silverton, Kaslo and Riondel. Forests were burned to search for minerals and cut for building railways and towns as well as for fuel. Rivers were dammed and Nelson and Sandon became the first towns in British Columbia with hydroelectric power. In this way, this rock is the source of even my presence in the region.

The past that had laid itself down, so precisely, so intricately, began to be unearthed. However, its value was not measured by the information it held or the spiritual glory it inspired, but rather through what it garnered, per gram, in the European stock markets. These rocks, these mountains were not seen as fundamental, influencing everything else that dwells here, but as wealth, the kind of wealth only money can buy. That many a soul risked his life and lost it for the promise of riches is another story, now embedded in the abandoned tunnels that riddle these mountains.

The drizzle intensifies and the fog closes around us, leaving only the glacier in view. It, like all of the other glaciers in the region, is shrinking, exposing barren ground, not unlike the ground revealed 10,000 years ago after icefields two kilometres deep retreated from this landscape. The fragmented rock that makes up the roadbed and rises in piles around us, known as moraines, is the work of this glacier. About 15,000 years ago, during the last glaciation, all this land, except perhaps the tips of the tall white peaks the fog has obscured from our view, were buried beneath thick ice. When the ice retreated, it left etchings and stories, grinding down rock, rounding valleys, depositing material, forming huge lakes and letting them go. The glaciers scraped the land off to its foundations. And it is from these foundations — their shapes, their mineral content, their aspect — that the land we now call home, complete with lush forests and wildlife, grew.

Rock is like an alphabet. When we sound out the shapes into letters, words, sentences, paragraphs and ideas, we begin to be able to read the land. Ecologist and wise man Stan Rowe was the first person to teach me the ABC's of glaciation. The previous summer, I had gone to see Stan in his New Denver home to talk about forests and fire, but he steered our conversation in the direction of landscapes and ecosystems. As an academic, a researcher and an integrator of ideas, Stan encouraged me to look beyond the "what" to the "why" and "how."

"Landforms are the Darwinian sieves that determine so much more. Landforms and watercourses left behind by glaciation set the stage for what will grow on individual sites," he told me. The foundations of what we see are grounded in the stories of rock and soil.

As we reach the lower edge of the glacier, which glows an ominous pale blue, I ask Martin to wait. I realize that I have never walked on a glacier before. And with climate change shrinking our glaciers at an unprecedented rate, I might not always have glaciers available for walking on. As I step up onto the hard but crumbling surface of the ice, I feel as though I'm doing something akin to climbing onto a horse's back. With all their retreating and advancing, pulsing and fracturing, these bodies of ice are alive. Like the mountains. Like rock.

My name suddenly takes on a new aura as I jump off the glacier onto hard rock ground. What my mother called stubbornness was perhaps only my childlike necessity to have things take their own time, and the strong integrity that my name has always implied to me is more flexible than I thought. Firm but subject to forces like every other object, live or dead. After all, time has its own agenda, one beyond our control, and it leaves its own marks imprinted inerasably in the landscape. If we learn to read them, we better understand our own place within the unfolding of time. We learn that the story continues. Even as I write these words, the present is slipping into the past, natural and human forces laying down their marks on the land.

Many days later, at home, I pick the chunk of galena off my living room windowsill. There, it has found a suitable groove to rest in on one of the gnome village rocks, among all the other rocks I have collected over the past 13 years. Since my trip to the Badshots, they all glow with a new intensity, a fresh mystery. As humans, we tend to think of ourselves as the endpoint of evolution, that the present, at least when it comes to the shape of the land, is fixed, its contents forever at our disposal. Especially rock. But mountain and rock, when we pay attention, tell us a story. It is a story of no special mystery, just the common magic of an Earth that is constantly transforming itself, a story with the heft of a glistening chunk of galena gathered from a crumbling mountain slope beneath the towering pillars of some ancient ocean floor and lit by another molten mass around which we spin and spin and spin.

Going Squirrely

K. Linda

I awake with a start in my tiny loft bedroom. What the . . . ? My heart pounds. I peer, still dreamy and confused, out the high window opposite my bed. The tops of the trio of large grand firs are faintly lit with the sparsest morning light. The sound bursts in my open window again. TSUK- TSUK-TSUK-Tsuk-TSUK!

It must be no more than four-effing-thirty. I climb out from under the covers to press my cheek against the window screen. The cool, late summer air feathers my nostril with the scent of forest sap and soil. The first birdsong of the day weaves into the rustling of boughs and leaves. But this is not what I'm after. Then I hear it: the faint scrape of claws on the cedar siding of my house on the outside of my bedroom wall.

"Buzz off!" I shout, banging on the inside of my wall. But this makes matters worse. TSUK-TSUKTSUK! TSUKTSUKTUSK! This barrage emanates a metre away. But now that I have intervened, the squirrel is as upset as I am. The scolding continues, more relentlessly now. On and on. I dive back into bed and cover my head with a pillow but the squirrel's pitch is calibrated to penetrate even feathers. Throwing the pillow at the window only cranks up the volume.

Eventually, the squirrel leaves and I fall back asleep. Later, over porridge and tea, I recall my morning tirade bashfully. The squirrel was only doing its squirrel thing. This is its home as much as mine. What's my problem? Don't I live in the woods to be close to that which is wild? I resolve to be more magnanimous.

When, the very next morning, I am awakened exactly the same way by this least tender of alarms imaginable, I realize what my problem is: the squirrel and I have conflicting needs. I need to sleep and it needs... What does it need? Surely it doesn't need my house. As I bury my head under two pillows, the TSUK-TSUK-TSUKTSUKT-SUKTSUKTSUK only somewhat muffled, it occurs to me that I've met up with one of those moments in a rural person's life where something needs to give: nature or me. When I first moved to the woods, I agonized over this. What right did I have to displace a mouse from my house, a noisy robin from my eaves, big black carpenter ants from my floor? With time, I became a participant in my homeplace rather than simply a voyeur and it became easier to take up some space. As a large mammal somewhere close to the top of the food chain, it's part of my role to eat and displace those further down the chain. As part of a species that has a tendency to consume at random and displace with gusto, I don't take this prerogative lightly, but I do take it. This is one of those times. Since I'm not going to move to accommodate the squirrel and don't plan to let the squirrel wreck every night's sleep for months to come, the squirrel has to go. The fact that squirrels are abundant and common here makes my decision easier. The question is, how to evict my unwanted tenant?

If I were to phone up CBC's First Nations comedy show, "The Dead Dog Cafe," and ask for an Indian name, my namers would have plenty of options. I am known for many things. Possibilities might be "All-walks-turn-into-bushwacks" or "Ideas-multiply-like-tapeworm" but if I had my say, I'd go down in the annals of history as "Catches-rodents-with-bare-hands." In a world that deals with unwanted rodents mostly through killing them, I consider my talent to be a relatively rodent friendly approach. To date, I've caught a ground squirrel, a couple of chipmunks, many deer mice, a wood rat and a flying squirrel, all with my hands. True enough, I had help cornering the wood rat and found the flying squirrel immobile under my couch; nevertheless, getting hold of these wily creatures of the forest is no mean feat. Nevertheless, I know that catching my unwanted dawn alarm clock will be the most difficult task of all.

Small and fierce, red squirrels thrive in the dense, moist coniferous forests of the Columbia Mountains. Most of the time, they are invisible, soft-shoeing it through the canopy of the trees above me, from swaying bough to swinging branch. But when one makes itself known, it is impossible to ignore. The red squirrel's distinctive tsuk-tsuk-tsuk! carries for hundreds of metres, even in the dim cedar, hemlock and fir woods around my home. Each angry tsuk! is accompanied by a twitch of the bushy red tail, a jerk of its tiny perfectly designed body, as if it takes more than just its voice box to emit this stupendous sound. Calibrated to a pitch designed to warn predators or competitors, a squirrel's voice nears perfection in the art of scolding.

The next morning, I am ready. As soon as her chatter erupts, I climb down the ladder out of my loft and slip out the door into the pearl grey of pre-dawn. I stand naked at the back of my house and gaze up at a scolding squirrel that clings to the siding. Her small body twitches in sharp, sparky movements as she stares down at me, the pink, gummy, furless big-head. Her cocky stance suggests the chutzpah of a being who knows she can go places where I cannot hope to follow. And I, "Catches-rodents-with-bare-hands," sigh, knowing I lack the ability to grab the wee beast as long as she is up high.

After some deliberation, I go out and buy a live trap.

Using organic peanut butter for bait, I catch the offending squirrel that night. The next morning, I drive five kilometres up a neighbouring logging road with a nervous, caged squirrel on the seat beside me. Local wisdom suggests this is the necessary distance to release a captured rodent so that it won't return. When I pop the metal door open, the squirrel leaps away in perfect grey-red arcs across the knapweed-infested shoulder of the road. I wish the squirrel well and drive back home, relieved that this debacle is over.

I have one morning of blissful, undisturbed sleep before squirrel #2 moves in.

TSUK-TSUK-TSUK! I say moves in but at this point, I begin to wonder what these squirrels are really doing on my house. My mammal guidebook informs me that red squirrels nest in trees, establishing territories varying in size from 0.2 to 1.0 hectares around their nest tree. Their food larders are usually in one midden, *in the ground*. Since my house is neither tree nor ground, my question remains unanswered.

That very day, I haul out the aluminum extension ladder and slide it open, against the back of my house. I discover chewed-through nylon mesh, which I stapled in place instead of the usual soffits to "protect" the insulated underside of my roof. I knock on the siding, not so much to be polite, but for fear the squirrel is still in there and might chomp on my hand. No response. I reach in gingerly and pat the prickly fibreglass, until my fingers encounter some hard objects. I cup my hand around them and pull them out. There, in my hand, is a wrinkled pile of tawny spheres that look like dried turds.

I puzzle over these feather-light, walnut-sized objects for some time. They are far too large to be squirrel turds, and when I break them open, they emit a pungent, familiar odour. I, like many people, suffer under the illusion that squirrels eat and store nuts. Pressed, I would add seeds to my list. It eventually dawns on me what these turds are: mushrooms! Once I get that far, I begin to identify boletes, puffballs, russula and others in the lot. Well I'll be.

Upon further investigation, I learn that red squirrels harvest mushrooms when they are available. Unlike northern flying squirrels, who also inhabit these forests and subsist on lichen and fungi, red squirrels only supplement their diets with mushrooms. Their prime food is conifer seeds. Cones. I have a moment of panic. Is my entire roof destined to be filled with cones? But no. Conifer cones need to be stored in moist ground to keep them from opening and spoiling. Mushrooms, on the other hand, need a dry larder. And what drier place than in my cozy, hand built house, protected by my new metal roof?

One puzzle remains: the mushrooms were already dry when the squirrel delivered them to my roof. Why? How? My neighbour Jake is the one who points out mushrooms to me, suspended from the branches of a small fir. "They hang them there to dry," he says.

"Any idea how many they store for one winter?" I ask. My runaway imagination has me waking up, buried in my bed by collapsed drywall and mounds of dried mushrooms. He has no answer. I climb back up that very day, doubling and tripling the mesh, as I staple the hole closed.

The next morning, squirrel #2 is back at work. I awake to its outraged squawking and scrambling on the siding when it discovers the route to its cache is blocked. Even though I should know better, I bang on the wall from the inside. It scolds louder, its TSUK-TSUK, TSUK-TSUK, TSUK-TSUK-TSUK-TSUK carrying among the trees. Sigh. After breakfast, I climb back up the ladder. The three layers of mesh have been chewed through. I put a mushroom in the live trap and set it on the ground near the base of the wall. I write "aluminum mesh" on my shopping list. Squirrel #2 wins an all expenses paid, one-way trip up beautiful Rover Creek, the very next day. I cover the cage with a towel, just in case, so it won't see where it's going.

As I pull open the cage, a rusty streak shoots out and, like squirrel #1, makes a beeline for the forested slope next to the road. Now that I've done some reading on their habits, I can't help but wonder how seriously I jeopardize this squirrel's survival by moving it away from its larders in early autumn. Red squirrels are highly territorial, and the size of their territories depends largely on the availability of food. When forest is logged, for example, the percentage of squirrels displaced is directly proportional to the percentage of timber volume cut. Researchers have yet to figure out what happens to the displaced squirrels. We do know they don't double up and share in moments of crisis. With the exception of a mother and her young, each territory has a single squirrel occupant. And because of stored foods, red squirrels have incredible site fidelity. They hang on, even in logged areas, until they run out of stored food before moving on.

As I go about my summer day, pulling chickweed, thistles and ferns out of the garden, going for a bracing swim in the Kootenay River down by the dams, I am pestered by the question of whether squirrel #2 will be able to establish a new territory and hoard enough food before winter arrives.

In the Columbia Mountains, squirrels are almost entirely reliant on stored food to survive the winter. Unlike mammals such as the porcupine, who has a lower critical body temperature in the winter, or the marten who grows significant fur cover or bears who fatten up and hibernate, the red squirrel is not physiologically adapted to cold. It relies on high food consumption to keep warm. One set of researchers estimated that one red squirrel needs approximately 13 bushels of Douglas fir cones or 24 bushels of lodgepole pine cones to survive a winter. Another study found that a single squirrel ate 123 to 176 spruce cones a day, or 35 pine cones and 639 buds off conifer trees! It is no wonder two-thirds of all red squirrels perish before they are a year old. Many die from starvation while others become food for a wide range of local forest predators including weasels, owls, goshawks and martens.

Squirrel #3 moves in a few days later. I realize then that we are experiencing a squirrel year, a population explosion that is pushing the limits of local squirrel territories. Like some other mammals, the most studied being the snowshoe hare, squirrel populations experience booms and busts. Based on a complex combination of factors, the most important of which is the success of the conifer seed crop, squirrel populations fluctuate from year to year. I speculate on the reasons for this year's boom (1998) as I climb the ladder to staple metal mesh over the holes as well as over all untouched mesh. I leave on a short trip. In my absence, squirrel #3 is found floating, drowned, in my rain barrel. Squirrel #4 is already on the job when I return.

I like squirrel #4 a lot. She is a quiet, diligent animal who doesn't scold much. In spite of this, I remain dedicated to evicting her. She shows up every morning, making numerous trips from the branches to eaves. I remount the ladder to discover she's chewed through the metal mesh. I rob her mushroom cache for bait and scheme to replace mesh with bits of wood. I set the trap. She is a smart squirrel, if such a thing can be humanly assessed. She learns to rob the live trap even when I sew dried mushrooms to the back of the cage. She evades me for weeks. I put a metal guard on the porch post that is her main transportation route up. A distinctive *ping* adds itself to the array of morning sounds. I smear a band of Vaseline on the posts and sprinkle them with cayenne pepper. Still squirrel climbs, still squirrel chews, still squirrel hoards.

By this time, I am thoroughly engaged in the life of this red squirrel. Coming from a rural northern culture, I understand in my very bones the flux between food availability and times of hunger. I relate to the necessity — and glee — of hoarding food. Friends who have but one box of pasta in the cupboard and a few shriveled vegetables in the fridge amaze me. How do they survive? "There's a 24 hour super-market just a block away," they offer in their defense.

Humans are primarily what Stephen Vander Wall, a hoarding behaviour expert, would call communal hoarders. Like beavers and honey bees, we have traditionally stored food with a group of "closely related individuals that maintain highly integrated social units persisting over long periods." I thought his definition of a communal larder as a "hub of activity for the group, a physical entity that acts to promote interactions and reinforce bonds among group members" described Nelson's food co-op perfectly.

Nevertheless, we are also a species prone to distrust. During the pre-Y2K madness, even one very sensible friend, who denied any fear of the predicted meltdown of society due to computer malfunction on New Year's Eve, decided to take preventive measures and hoard some food. He was still eating dried beans from that era four years later. Maybe because rural people tend to hoard food seasonally, canning and freezing fruit and vegetables from their gardens and the wilds, Y2K hoarding flourished more here than in the cities. This flame of hoarding was certainly fanned by a local tendency toward discussing and propagating conspiracy theories. In the Slocan Valley, some dug up their yards with backhoes to squirrel away 14-year supplies of nitrogen-preserved food. Candles, batteries, canning jars and lids, were stocked and restocked on hardware store shelves. The Y2K preparedness store, capitalizing on people's unease, did bracing sales in generators and survival gear.

At home, we traded a gas barrel for wheel alignment and filled and kept a second barrel for ourselves. I bought a Swede saw and a shovel, rationalizing that these were, after all, items I would use in any case. Much less immediately useful stuff was hoarded in those days as well. By mid-February, after the disaster that never was, people tried to unload thousands of pairs of mitts and tens of solar panels they had purchased to use as trade items after the collapse. But beans get hard after a few years.

In the language of animal behaviour, squirrels are larder hoarders — individual animals tend to concentrate their stored food at one site. For red squirrels, this takes the form of a cone midden underground. Cones are buried in groups of 20 to 40 in multiple chambers in the accumulated cone debris. There's one under the big hemlock southwest of my house. The mounded earth of the forest floor is dotted with dozens of holes around a half-rotten log. Bits of cones, rusty red against the mossy earth, encircle each hole. Though I sometimes sit and wait, crouched a discrete and shadowed distance away, I've never seen a squirrel come or go.

Storing food only gives an animal the advantage if the individual gets to eat what it hoarded. Larder hoarding seems, in most circumstances, to be the key element in the squirrel's defense success. Red squirrels spend much of their time scolding and chasing away neighbouring squirrels and other animals.

This is where the squirrels at my house went wrong. How do

they make the crucial choices between slipping quietly through the forest and making an attention-grabbing racket? If I were a weasel instead of a gummy sluggish beast, would they pester me so? I probably would have slept through their morning hoarding expeditions had they not insisted on waking me up. Clearly, they knew little about the mental workings of this human.

Squirrel #4 continues to elude me. I relocate the live trap and intensify my capture plan. I climb up to the roof only to discover that the squirrel has pushed aside one of the pieces of wood I had inset into its entrance hole. I go for glue.

If hoarding is such a supreme strategy, I wonder as I climb up the ladder for the umpteenth time, why don't all animals in wintry places hoard food? Hoarders not only secure a food supply for times of scarcity, they also increase their chances of survival through being able to make "time management" decisions, like when to court instead of forage, when to hide out instead of risk being eaten, when to plump up the offspring and hang around instead of scrambling to feed hungry bellies in the moment of need.

So, why do the local osprey wing it down to the Baja while the hawks and owls store up rows of mice? Why do deer and elk perish in the deep snow while the small high alpine pika is busy nibbling at its hay bale? Why do snowshoe hares leave themselves open to becoming lynx snacks while squirrels suck mushrooms in the safety of their nests? What caused squirrels #1 through #4 to be so incredibly dedicated to hoarding that none of my antics could deter them?

Stephen Vander Wall's book presents numerous hypotheses for the evolution of hoarding behaviour. He suggests that overlapping circumstances cause hoarding behaviour to emerge in a species. Two conditions must be present however: the fitness of the hoarder must exceed that of a non-hoarder; and an animal must have some kind of genetically-based food handling behaviour that creates the preconditions for hoarding. For example, if a squirrel that snags a mushroom off the forest floor, then rushes to a safe place to munch on it happens to abandon it, it creates an opportunity for itself to find the food later. If the food is found intact, a by-the-way circumstance may become purposeful. In other words, animals who recover morsels left behind are the most likely to keep leaving them behind. And find better ways to leave food behind. No point in filling your fridge with chocolate if your housemate is premenstrual. The sock drawer? Or the sock drawer and the pocket of your jacket in your closet? Safely hidden, now all you — they — have to do is remember where you hid the stuff.

The red squirrel has solved, in a relatively simple way, the quandary of how to relocate food it has stored. Tuck the food mostly in one place and guard it. If anyone approaches, bombard them with verbal abuse. This is not to say that squirrels have little memory, however. The fact that squirrel after squirrel took over the mushroom cache in my roof suggests that squirrels use their memory capabilities for noting where their neighbours are storing food. In fact, mother squirrels have been observed appropriating a vanished neighbour's midden and territory to pass on to one of its kits when it matures. We often think of memory and planning as human attributes, indications of our intelligence. Yet, hoarding behaviour in animals, whether you label it instinct or not, suggests that we are not alone in our ability to take stock of the past and make reasoned plans for the future.

A case in point is squirrel #4. Smart beast that she is, she figures out the working of my live trap enough to continue robbing it for three weeks, well into autumn. She eludes capture like an old-west outlaw. Instinct or intelligence, I don't know, but she's a survivor. She still scrambles up the siding but I conclude she's no longer able to get in under my roof. This is not for lack of trying, though. I monitor the progress of her chewing on the wood pieces I glued into my roof gaps carefully but at an inch thick, her work is slow. The longer the bushy-tailed bandit evades me, the more I secretly cheer her on. But only part of me is soft-hearted; the trap remains baited and ready.

One chill morning in late September, I awake to the startling absence of fine claws on the cedar siding. I hurry downstairs and out the door to check the trap. I lift the camouflaging cedar boughs off the cage and, sure enough, the squirrel is there, curled up at one end. Success! At long last! I lift the cage to eye level. Asleep? No: dead.

But no! I shake the cage. This is a *live* trap. LIVE. My desperation gives way to grief. I have killed Super Squirrel, the smartest rodent in the Columbia Mountains. And beautiful too. I reach in and lift her cold body out. The white ringed eyes are closed. Her pale belly unmarked. Her reddish-grey fur and tail soft and intact. Did she die of fright? Did the door wing shut in such a way as to injure her? Was the night too cool for her to survive outside her nest? Or?

We bury squirrel #4 in a shallow hole behind my house along an old skid trail that small fuzzy hemlocks are re-inhabiting. I make a cedar marker for her grave, inscribing it with "R.I.P. a mighty fine squirrel, 1998." I call my land partners Joe and Christopher down for the funeral. During the "service" I talk about my conflict with the squirrels and offer my apologies to the dearly departed. I ask the other squirrels to leave my eaves alone. I call for a truce. No hymns are sung but after I push the dirt back over the hole, Joe and I sob on each other's shoulders. Chris watches us with some puzzlement, wondering how he ended up participating in this peculiar drama.

I visit the grave every day for a few weeks, then about once a week until the snow comes. No new squirrel moves in but when once I barely noticed squirrels, now the forest is full of them, their harvested cones falling about me like heavy rain, their middens reminding me of my half-filled root cellar. They greet me as I sit by the creek in my morning meditation, they chatter on fallen trees as I sit watching loggers cut holes in the forest, they leap through the air above me as I gather tea herbs in the woods, they eye me as I pull long, fat parsnips out of the garden earth. Together, we busily prepare for winter, their early morning forays inspiring me to get on with the necessary work. Our lives are tightly woven into the fabric of these forested mountains, forever showing me how my territory overlaps with that of so many other creatures, seen and unseen. I hold this knowledge in my heart, like a middle name, to remind me of the first civilizing lessons that we are taught as children: how to live with those around us.

The Snow, The Snow

Vine Maple
laden w/ snow.

elp

K.Linda

It is completely silent on Meadow Mountain. The fine, softly falling snow has interrupted the wind, enveloping the sparse trees like fog. It is so still; each breath hangs in the air, surrounding me with ghost-like apparitions. The spruces, white-robed wizards, appear out of the fog as I move forward. The light is so flat that what remains of green blends into a black and white spectrum. Most is pearly grey. Only the deep wells around the tree trunks add darker gradations. The snow must be two metres thick. Though I am wearing cross-country skis, this classic Kootenay snow is so dry, so light, I am immersed to my waist. There is no gliding here, just plowing through the feathery soup, step by step. The snow rustles faintly as it lets me pass.

Five — or was it 10? — minutes ago, I encountered some birds flittering and chittering from tree to tree. There are no other signs of animal life, no tracks in the snow, no whistling, howling or peeping, no animals scurrying for shelter. Yet I know they are here. While the bears and other hibernators have opted for the sleep-and-let-it-pass option, the lynx, hare, wolverine, squirrel, owl, porcupine, weasel, marten, as well as grouse and ptarmigan, voles and mice, insects and spiders are living waking lives like me. They are all here, above or below the snow, somehow finding food, warmth and refuge. To endure this austere and harsh environment is nothing short of miraculous to me. How long would I survive here?

Without a pack and the necessities of survival — water, food, extra clothing — I suddenly feel naked. When I came to visit my land partner Christopher at the lodge where he drives a snowcat every winter, I hadn't counted on ending up high in the mountains. The plan had been to laze around the lodge and do a little cross-country skiing, but when it became apparent he needed to work on some snowroads for the upcoming week's skiing, I threw my skis in the back of the enormous machine. When we found the area where he was to pack down some road, he suggested I go on ahead. My departure from the snowcat seems like it was hours ago. Christopher assured me he would follow soon. But what if I took a wrong turn? I listen now intently for the churning noise it was such a relief to escape. As the snow continues to envelope me, my exhilaration and awe begin to give way to panic. The lodge is kilometres away beyond avalanche prone slopes and the valley bottom farther still. What would this bone-numbing snow make of me? I close my eyes, breathe deeply and attempt to return to the sweet country of silence and awe. The snow is so sound absorbent; the snowcat is almost upon me before I hear its deep roar. I turn to see the tank-like machine bearing down on me, its eyes blaring bright.

Relief. Regret. I climb up into the warm cab. Chris turns to me and grins. I smile back, safe now. He sets the machine in motion and the snow parts before us, like a Biblical sea. Here is the bulk of what earns the Columbia Mountains region its unique designation as the Interior Temperate Rainforest. As the snow rushes at the windscreen, I think: *shouldn't that be snowforest then?*

Eileen

I have heard the snowfalls of the Columbia Mountains classified as abundant. This seems paradoxical to me. As someone born and raised in a Mediterranean climate, abundance connotes fruitfulness to me. Snow, on the other hand, falls at a lifeless time in the landscape's heave and sigh of seasons. It falls in enormous drifts, yes. But on a terrain made still with winter death, a landscape which has shut down its own abundance of flora and fauna, how can this mountain shroud be considered abundant?

After many years here, I have learned that the trick of the snow's abundance rests in its transformation. Snow does not remain snow throughout the year. When it begins to melt, it converts from ice crystals to liquid, which runs down the mountains to the valleys or soaks slowly into the thawing soil.

The Columbia Mountains are a region of water, with countless streams, several rivers and sizable lakes strung along lush mountain valleys. Sometimes, in February, when I am tired of shovelling a path and tired of the cold, I remind myself that the spring and summer's gush of liquid is made possible by winter snowfall. The heavy drifts accumulating in the alpine from September to June, melt slowly through the hot months. Snow is a remarkable natural reservoir. The gradual melt feeds the streams and rivers, the lakes and the water table, as the thaw line rises from the valley bottoms to the subalpine ridges to the alpine and the glaciers.

By the end of March, the snow has disappeared from my valley-bottom garden. I see or think little of it until November, when one day, I smell an urgency in the wind whipping off the lake. The light feels ominous and the sky unusually heavy. This, my instincts tell me, is my last day to touch the bare ground. I know without words that the arriving storm will seal the soil off from my hands for several months. Despite the fact that I have lived most of my life in warmer climates, I still know how to prepare. I scurry through the wind, rushing to complete outdoor tasks, raking leaves into the compost and planting a few last bulbs. The next morning, the ground is indeed gone. My relationship with the Earth has been transformed.

K. Linda

Some people welcome this transformation, others fear it. Few people of the snowy Columbias are neutral on the subject.

Up until a few years ago, I didn't welcome snow. I was what ecologists would call a chionophobe, an organism not adapted to snow. Oh sure, I tobogganed and skied, skated and snow-forted like a good northern child, but I was always relieved when it was all over and I could be inside. Like a cat, I'd curl up in some warm, soft place and gaze out, eyes half-lidded, at the snowy yard. Coming from a far northern culture, I was slightly ashamed of my discomfort with winter. It seemed to indicate weakness or, at least, a certain lack of hardiness.

Here in the Columbias, through living intimately with snow, I have come to appreciate winter. In my mountainside home, with its winter walk-in access and, for many years, no electricity, the stalemate between me and the snow has ended. Trammeled slush has given way to clean white footpaths and the glistening ice sculptures of a mountain creek. Cold, gloomy streets have been replaced by snow-shrouded forest and silvery moonlit mountains. The crackling of a wood fire has silenced the blast of the forced-air furnace. Winter is also a time of rest from gardening, wood gathering, building and the hundreds of other jobs that cease the moment the snow flies. It is a time to nurse injuries, revive the imagination and intellect, spend time with friends, go and do for no purpose other than pleasure or curiosity. Miraculously, at least psychologically, I had somehow adapted to winter, becoming a chioneuphore, an organism not adapted to snow but able to survive nevertheless.

Eileen

I only became well acquainted with snow in my mid-thirties, when our family moved to the Columbia Mountains. I never really spent any time in a snowy landscape before that, other than a few years in New England. I had no concept, until well into adulthood, of what it would be like to live in a landscape where moisture captured by mountains and Arctic air would dress the ground with fluff that, in its surprising density, could hold my weight. The first time I took a toboggan down a slope at the age of 35, snow crept up the back of my sweater onto bare skin and I rose up from the ground with white stuff stuck to every inch of my fleece pants. It has taken more than a few years to learn how to shake off the snow and trudge up the hill again. My sons do not seem to be affected by the cold white seeping in over the tops of their boots or the speed of the toboggan as it whisks through the cold air. They have a brave and knowing attitude toward snow that I envy. They understand with the flick of their fingers through accumulated flakes which type is best for skiing, which for tobogganing, which for packing a snowball. This is knowledge I have not passed on to them.

I cannot say I like snow. I have developed a respect for it. And I am learning to appreciate the spare visual beauty of a winter vista, to be out in it, finding my way on skis. I have an affinity for the paradoxes inherent in the form and physics of snow. It can be soft and hard. Light and heavy. Thick and thin. Cold and warm. It freezes and it insulates. It compacts and it fluffs. It is harsh, and yet softly beautiful. It is both secretive in what it hides and open-faced in what it presents to the world.

K. Linda

So what of those people who claim to love winter and snow? The snowcat, which is designed to bring such people here, negotiates the forested snowy slope in front of me. I wonder if it is winter we love or the context snow provides us for sport and adventure. After all, what do the powder pigs and piston heads know about snow itself? About flakes and facets, about its prodigious storage of water, about crystals and grains, about the mechanics of avalanches, about the ecology of winter, about the nutrients snow supplies to the Earth? Most of the people who come to the expensive winter lodge we are slowly angling toward, think of snow primarily in terms of influence. Caught up in feelings — usually glee, if they're skiers — they, and many others, overlook the fundamentals. As winter ecologists have discovered, "it is only under the most pressing of circumstances that the human species accepts the degree of prolonged exposure necessary to successfully acclimatize to the cold. . . . By our cultural and technological ingenuity, we have exploited the coldest places on earth. Biologically, however, we remain essentially tropical beings."

Animals and plants move into wintry places like the Columbia Mountains and adapt to deep snow over many generations. This is a long process, a very long process that we, as humans, have only begun. As the last glaciers melted leaving a rocky, barren ground, the ability of an organism to adapt to the cold and snow was a make-or-break factor in whether it re-inhabited this area. And though the climate of the region has had its ups and downs, from the warm hypsithermal which scientists place anywhere from 5,000 to 8,000 years ago, to the "little ice age" somewhere between 1450 and 1850, to the climate change occurring now, a plant's or animal's ability to respond to the Columbia winter is key to its survival.

The machine's thrumming progress through the snow-hunched trees has lulled me into a contemplative half-sleep. The windshield wipers beat out a steady rhythm to this mechanical music. I peer out now, hoping to see a grouse huddling under a tree, in a burrow, upon a branch, shaking away the heavy snow, shrugging the cold from its small body. One small gesture — be it to fly away, to gather food, to gorge on berries then throw a paw over one's eyes and attempt to forget it all — turns the wheel of evolution. There is no turning it back. Few transformations have an end, except perhaps extinction. Some animals evolve not just to tolerate or survive snow, but to rely on it. They are called chionophiles. Even small changes to the snowpack, a year of tremendous snow or one of scarcity, can throw a monkey wrench into this survival strategy. So much depends on snow.

Eileen

January. The wind howls across the hillside out my studio window. I have not seen the bare ground for two months. My favourite sweater reeks of wood smoke from a daily fire to keep my studio warm enough for writing. Thirsty, but too lazy to trudge through the snow to the house for a drink, I fill a mayonnaise jar from the snow outside my door and place it on the woodstove. Within minutes, the jar of opaque solid has melted into a thin pool of clear liquid covering no more than one centimetre at the bottom of the glass which was once full to the brim. I have had a Columbia Mountain epiphany: snow is mostly air.

I have always thought of snow as something dense that can be held in the palm, packed into a ball, weighted on a shovel. Snow is a solid form of precipitation, a mass of moisture and air that piles onto tree stumps, settles delicately on berries still clinging to bare branches, smoothes the late-autumn tatter of gardens. Like clothing, it covers the bare, sometimes lumpy or wrinkled skin of the landscape, makes it look perfect. But the rapid disappearance of the solid, white mass from my mayonnaise jar reminds me that snow is only putting on an act. It isn't as tangible as it seems.

Sometimes, riding the ski lift at the edge of the alpine with my son, we lift gloved hands up into the falling sky to catch a few flakes. Against the black leather of my mitten, I can see how much snow depends on air for its substance. Each flake of the millions falling around me is composed of tiny hair-like ice crystals linked loosely to form larger units. From afar, these flakes look like ruffled white planets tumbling to the ground. But, on my glove and against my warm tongue, density melts instantly into intricacy. A snowflake is a sphere that is not a sphere. Air that is not air, a cold moment torn from the clouds and sent by gravity toward the ground.

Snow protects ice. That may seem to be a paradox, but ice is an important commodity here. Gradual melt from glaciers provides almost three-quarters of the region's average river flow in August. The few remaining glaciers sprinkled around the alpine reaches of the Monashee, Selkirk and Purcell ranges shrink as the effects of global warming reduce their size. Snow melts more slowly than the dense and often dark weight of the glacial ice. Snow that has fallen on top of glaciers protects them from rapid melt through the long hot summer.

Snow is mostly air, cold air caught high in the clouds, then torn from them and sent by gravity toward the ground. The geometric structure of crystallized water holds the air in place as the flakes tumble to the Earth.

K. Linda

As the snowcat chugs into its bay in the lodge's enormous shed and Christopher shuts down the engine, I jump out eager to return to the quietude of the snow. Outside, I hold my face up to the sweet sting of the falling flakes and realize that the lodge's generator is blaring away. I retrieve my skis from the back of the snowcat and set off at a good clip.

Lovely as this weekend adventure is, the irony of lodges like this does not escape me. On one hand, North Americans are becoming increasingly dependent on fossil fuels for everything, including recreation. Burning fossil fuels creates climate change which, in the Columbia Mountains, has already amounted to an annual increase in temperature of 1.1 degrees C. This influences the size of the snowpack as well as the timing and peaks of water flow in the creeks and rivers of the area. Watershed by watershed, the microclimate is shifting, altering centuries-old precipitation patterns — when precipitation falls and what it falls as, rain or snow. What will become of this ecosystem if snow teeters in the balance?

It's hard to picture the postcard perfect Meadow Mountain slopes above and below me bereft of snow. The ground here is blanketed in deep powder for up to 10 months of each year and, in most years, so abundantly that small trees that dot the slope must live decades before their needles are exposed to winter light and winter cold. Once the ground is buried under 40 to 50 centimetres of snow, the temperature below the snow is almost constant. Hibernators depend on a good snow cover to keep their dens and hibernacula warm. Plants of all varieties depend on snow to prevent the freezing of their roots, corms, bulbs and even above-ground segments. At home, in the winter of 2000-2001 for example, we lost the carrots we habitually overwinter in their garden beds when a sharp spell of cold arrived before the snow. In the spring, they were spongy globs of brown instead of the golden nuggets of sweetness we had come to rely on. What other plants were damaged? Which animals shivered desperately in their hideaways, hoping for snow? What insects, larvae, pupae and eggs, are below this snow, counting on it to keep them from freezing?

The lodge disappears from view; all is quiet again except for the swish of my skis against the snow. Christopher's daily ski trail is covered by 10 centimetres of new snow, but his tracks are obvious. As I enter a copse of trees, I slow my stride to look for the air holes made by the small mammals who spend the winter scurrying below. What pikas, shrews, voles, weasels and others are busy tunneling winter roads beneath this apparently lifeless shroud? Their small bodies and quick metabolisms demand snow. Without it, they wouldn't survive the harsh cold.

Below snow, in snow, through snow, on snow. I strike off on a road spur that has no tracks and quickly sink up to my knees. I recall this afternoon's floundering in deep snow, struggling for every forward movement, and decide to turn back. Most winter animals are better designed for snow travel than I. Both ptarmigan and grouse grow special feathers on their feet, not unlike hemlock boughs, to create a snowshoe effect that keeps them aloft on snow. Grouse also grow special spurs on their legs for the winter. The spurs help them grip onto icy branches, where they spend their days foraging, and to dig into the snow quickly when they do their famous flying dives into snowdrifts. Thus ensconced, the birds nestle in for a cozy sleep unless someone — like me — comes along and disturbs them. Then, they erupt from the snow like a bomb going off.

I stop to catch my breath and pull off my toque. The clamour of the lodge has completely faded; even the birds are quiet here. The snow, which so beautifully blankets the branches, berries and ground around me is, for many birds, a dangerous shroud. Most birds resist cold well if there is an abundance of food; however, the snow can quickly cover up food sources. It's not surprising that of bird species that overwinter in the West Kootenay, all must find and adapt to above-snow sources of food. Nuthatches are thought to have evolved their distinctive ability to hang around upside down on branches due to their winter need to forage on the bottoms of snow-laden branches. The ubiquitous chickadee has been discovered to grow a larger brain in the fall to store much needed memories of where it has cached seeds. Chickadees survive low temperatures by lowering their own body temperature to a closely regulated hypothermia. When their temperature drops to 10 degrees F below their normal, they experience a 20 percent saving in energy. Nuthatches and wrens, on the other hand, are noted for squishing themselves into communal nests to share body heat. Up to 60 wrens have been found in one nest!

I stand quietly for many minutes as snowflakes embed themselves in my hair. Finally cool again, I tug my toque back down over the tops of my ears. The captured flakes melt and tingle against my scalp. If I were a wolverine, one of the best adapted winter mammals of the Columbias, I would simply shake myself and the ice in my fur would slide gloriously off in a tinkling heap. The wolverine's winter fur, which is of a texture and oily slipperiness that increases its insulation value, is ideal for this snow.

The bedded strata of Columbia snow also provides the wolverine opportunities for satiating its appetite. The wolverine hangs around the bases of avalanche chutes where it benefits from the hapless moose, caribou or mountain goats who swept away by rivers of snow. What it cannot eat, it caches in the preserving cold of the snow and returns to eat again and again. Its powerful jaws have evolved to be able to crunch through both bones and frozen meat.

My vegetarian stomach growls in response to this very carnivorous thought. I glide to a halt and throw one ski in the opposite direction, executing a 180 degree turn. When I follow up with the other ski, its tip catches and I plunge, limbs askew, into the snow beside the trail. I sink and flounder to get up as if drowning. Oh, for the wolverine's ability to travel with ease on snow! I thrash about, trying to prop myself up with my poles and muscle my way to a standing position. The wolverine's 13 kilogram bulk is spread out over wide, oily-furred paws. Where ungulates, canines, most felines and humans with limited skiing abilities like me tend to sink, the wolverine skates. A long, wide creature, it moves like a travelling wave on legs.

I should probably be in the valley bottom along with deer, elk and moose. Like me, they flounder once the powdery snow is a metre deep. Even when the snow glazes over hard enough for me to stroll across its glimmering surface — which it does fairly reliably around my house sometime in February — the heavy-bodied elk or deer break through, the shards of ice cutting and injuring their legs. Does it ever get hard enough to hold them aloft? Do they test it, like me, placing one careful step after the other, thinking "be light, be light!"? Do they, like me, curse as the crust collapses suddenly beneath one wrongly placed step?

Finally, I resort to taking off my skis to get up. Being mired in snow cuts the pleasure of snow very quickly. And more than that, it makes survival difficult. Hence: snowshoes, toboggans, skis, snow-boards, snowmobiles, snowcats and helicopters. But we humans are alone in being able to consciously alter our physical adaptability to snow. And herein lies the tragedy of our love of snow.

As I stride back toward the lodge, I notice that the wind has picked up, driving snow into my face. A fierce storm is blowing in. Snow devils swirl around the lodge and the branches unload their burdens. It could be a big dump, Columbia Mountain style. Tomorrow's incoming guests are perhaps dancing with glee at the thought of fresh powder on these slopes. The deer and elk, with neither houses nor devices, turn their butts to the wind, put their heads down and chew the cud.

Until recently, the high snowy ridges of places like Meadow Mountain were places where people did not go in the winter but the boom in backcountry winter sports has disrupted the winter's peace for the animals who tough it out here. Snowmobilers, skiers, helicopters and snowcats now plow through the snowy alpine. Ski lodge proposals continue to sprout, from Jumbo to Snowwater Creeks, but many of those who make use of these recreational opportunities remain oblivious of their impact.

I arrive at the rumbling lodge and stand outside to hold my face up to the blustering cold for one last minute. My adaptations to this place are all external to me; shelters and devices allow me to enter winter in ways that have taken other animals countless generations to evolve. Though these devices allow me and other human beings to exploit winter, they do not make us part of it. Not here, not like this. I wipe a drip from my nose and head indoors to gather my towel. Somewhere, a hot tub awaits me.

Slow to Perfection

K. Linda

    It's a wintry day on the land, a slow day, the kind that brings out the cozymeister in me. The snow falls steadily, wrapping the trees in downy cloaks, erasing all traces of hares, dogs, humans and other animals from the ground. Indoors, at the Big House, a fire crackles in the bulky wood stove that, with the coming of the autumn cool, becomes the centrepiece of my land partners' living room. Joe reads by the picture window in the rocking chair her grandfather built. Jessie putters in the kitchen singing. A guest is sprawled on the couch reading, and I watch the snow tumble, white against the backdrop of white clouds and white mountains. The fragrances of wood, both freshly chopped and burning, permeate the high-ceilinged room.

When a faint buzzing adds itself to the array of homey sounds, no one except the guest looks up. No one except the guest — who may be from the east or west, or south or just a city, but not from here — pays any attention to the brownish insect with the dangling abdomen and legs that flies across the room, ending its trajectory by bumping into a lamp next to the couch.

"Euwww," the guest calls out. "What is it? Yuck."

"Just Geoffrey," I answer. I watch the guest shrink back from the insect that has landed on the wooden back of the massive, slab-wood couch and has begun walking, ever so slowly, in his direction. Jessie notices the guest's distress and takes pity.

"It's just a cedar bug. It won't hurt you. They don't bite, get into the food, or anything. They're inoffensive. They just like to come indoors for the winter and when the room warms up, they fly around."

"But they're so big...."

For sure, being the size of an elongated dime makes *Leptoglossus occidentalis* a conspicuous insect. As a member of the Hemipteran or "true bug" family, it has a notable triangle on its thorax and a very buggish appearance. Though its random flights across rooms draw people's attention, mostly it likes to sit on furniture probing the air in looping circles with its long antennae, while its distinctively bent-kneed legs stick well out from its boxy body. All told, the cedar bug is not bad looking, but if someone has never encountered one before, it does have a certain docile fierceness to its features.

"Aren't you going to get rid of it?" the guest wants to know.

We laugh, not unkindly, each remembering the hundreds of cedar bugs we have escorted outside or otherwise disposed of, only to find there are hundreds more to replace them. Each bug is seemingly identical, thus, my land partner Karen's generic name of Geoffrey for all cedar bugs. Its official common name is western conifer seed bug.

Though next to no one local uses this name, it is more accurate since the bug has no special predilection for cedar trees.

"It'll move out in the spring on its own," I answer.

The guest, clearly dissatisfied, makes a move, as if to crush the bug who is now marching in slow-motion across the back of the couch, lifting each of the three legs on either side of its body one at a time. Even on perfectly smooth, flat surfaces, cedar bugs lift their legs high and place their feet carefully, with almost clownish precision. A local guitarist once made up a piece to go with its distinctive walk, called the "Cedar Bug Boogie."

"NO!!" the three of us call out in unison as the guest's arm lifts in a very familiar gesture. "Don't kill it. It'll smell. They're also known as stink bugs."

"I thought you said they're inoffensive."

I wander over to the couch and give Geoffrey a practiced flick. It flies off languidly, buzzing, and crashes into the window. I am pleased it has not circled back, as they sometimes do, only to collide with the person who performed the flick. Many people, who encounter the bugs on a regular basis, have learned to perfect the cedar bug flick, middle finger trigger released from behind the thumb in a pointed, swooping gesture. If you get it right, the bug flies off instead of releasing its distinctively acrid odour.

"They're fine as long as you leave them alone," I tell the guest who watches all this with some amazement. As I slouch back into the La-Z-Boy by the fire, I decide not to tell him about the infamous cedar bug that fell into a friend's popcorn, which she was distractedly eating while transfixed by a television screen. We are all familiar with the gesture: dip, toss in the mouth, chew. It would not pay for the guest to know about the popcorny crunchiness of a cedar bug and the fact that one tastes as bad as it stinks.

No, there are many things we do not tell strangers about Geoffrey. As the winter companion to our lives that it is, Geoffrey's arrival indoors is a yearly rite of passage. A mark in time to incite us to finish harvesting the garden, to get supplies in, to prepare for the snowing in of the driveway we do not plow, to hunker down for our slower, more contemplative winter lives. The first cedar bugs are potent enough signs that we speak of their arrival to each other. Their appearance indoors evokes wistful smiles or panic depending on how far along we are with our winter preparations or how desperate we are to return to our inner lives. Having neglected to speak of Geoffrey since its departure in the spring, we return suddenly to our thoughts and stories of it and of our winter selves.

We rarely share our Geoffrey stories with those not in-the-know. Stories and naming it, after all, represent our desire to be at peace with the creature. Once we came to understand that cedar bugs would arrive in the autumn, some years in tremendous numbers, and stay until spring, stories were our way of plowing through our distaste and fear in order to co-exist with them. The guest, however, has no reason, no yearly incentive, to overcome his distaste.

I remember a time when I was disgusted by them. One winter, I collected all the plodding cedar bugs in my newly constructed house into a glass jar. One by one, I'd sweep them off the tables, lampshades, kitchen counter and windowsill and drop them in the jar where they lay, day after day, in a tangled heap of interlocking legs. I poked no holes in the metal lid. I shut it tight and let the mass of them suffocate. Where did this deliberately murderous impulse come from?

Such cruelty regarding cedar bugs is, unfortunately, not unusual. Joe, who is immersed in her astrology books against the backdrop of the snowy day, looks up to tell me about vacuuming up hundreds of bugs. In the slanting February sunlight, the blue room of the lakeside cabin she was living in glowed from the reflection of the sun on both snow and water. The cedar bugs had emerged en mass from some unknown crevice in the room and her urge to clean up their "psychological stink" overrode any wonder. One local artist, a gentle man who will remain nameless, used cedar bugs in his paintings but it was not to extol their beauty. He dipped them in paint and let them stroll on his canvas until they died, congealed to the surface in crimson, cadmium yellow or thallo blue.

What has Geoffrey ever done to us to merit such maltreatment? Why revere the flutter and delicacy of butterflies, marvel at the iridescent colours of dragonflies, admire the keen skim of water striders and be repulsed by a simple bug? After all, they are all insects. Perhaps such dislike is based in suspicion, suspicion in fear, fear from lack of knowledge. Children and entomologists aside, we relegate the insect world far from the centre of what we value. We fashion our monsters and aliens after them: bug-eyed, many-limbed, possessing unknown senses and exhibiting behaviours that make us squirm. But unlike most monsters and aliens, they enter our homes and want to live at our sides, even on us. Do we, as human beings, have a genetic predisposition to shirk their touch or is this a learned behaviour?

I get up from my comfy La-Z-Boy and wander over to the windowsill where a small congregation has formed. Now that I know more about them, they are no longer ugly or distasteful to me. A bit of information has opened my mental door to fascination. The six bugs on the windowsill are fine representatives of their species, each standing alert and firm. As I eye them, I realize that although I cohabit with cedar bugs for half of every year, I haven't really observed them, taken the time to see them. This may be, in part, because watching cedar bugs who are coasting in and out of inertia is about as exciting as watching a game of chess. Though they wake up when the room

75

warms up, most of the winter they exist in the reduced metabolic state known as torpor or diapause, where their critical body temperature declines with the temperature, allowing them to preserve energy and to survive without food. Hence, we have the discrepancy between the biologists' characterization of *Leptoglossus occidentalis* as an "active insect" and people's experience of Geoffrey as the slow-motion king.

I have a hard time imagining cedar bugs in their full, warm season glory. But, as Thomas Lowe Fleischner points out, "The naturalist's task transcends the obvious. Not only must one sharpen eye and ear to perceive nuances . . . [but] the naturalist must attempt something even harder: to see the unseen.... Only through constant scrutiny — using all senses, as well as the imagination — can the naturalist begin to have a sense of . . . story."

I drop my head to eye-level with the windowsill to get a better look. Previously, their perpetually bent legs, showy antennae, and the notable patterns on their backs and wings had absorbed all my notice. Now I hone in on the head. It is small and rounded, like the tip of a well-used pencil, with eyes set on either side, back close to the body. The antennae are attached close to the tip. For the first time, I notice the oft-mentioned sucking proboscis that is the mouth, its feeding tool; its slender length is tucked under the body, extending halfway to the other end. I have never seen a cedar bug eat! This small, tucked away appendage is powerful enough to pierce through cone scales and seed husks alike and yet, for most of the year, it rests unused, neatly concealed.

Or nearly unused. Gale Ridge O'Connor, a biologist who did her masters thesis on the western conifer seed bug, observed the bugs spending a large part of their day grooming and that the procedure they use to clean each part of their bodies is meticulous. I try to see how, according to her description, the bug places its proboscis in the joint between its tibia and the first segment of its leg in order to secure the appendage while it strokes and cleans it. My friends on the windowsill, however, are barely moving. Only one is grooming, rubbing its long, unusually shaped back leg with the middle leg, over and over. The upper segment of the hind leg seems to have a jagged edge, whereas the next, the tibia, flattens and flares out in the leaf shape that is the source of the bug's Latin genus, *Leptoglossus*, meaning leaf-footed. Once it stops, my attention drifts to another cluster of cedar bugs, some of them dead, who occupy the space between the two windowpanes.

This past winter, my friends Allison and Mark reported a congregation of dozens of cedar bugs on the pull string of a light in the centre of their living room. "They're all clustered there in a glob. It's pretty intense. Why do they do that?"

"Aggregation pheromone," I told Allison as she attempted to control the disgusted twitch of her lip. "The males put out this chemical so that the others can find them." *Leptoglossus occidentalis* is, after all, considered "gregarious." As the insect passes through its five developmental stages, known as instars, to adulthood, only in the second instar phase does it *not* emit the pheromone designed to draw its pals around. Gale Ridge-O'Connor theorized that this might be the stage at which the bug disperses in the forest to find food and to mix up its genetics.

Ridge-O'Connor also noticed that there seemed to be a tendency toward group activities among them. When hot, groups of cedar bugs will flash their wings at the same time. If one individual does it, holding its wings away from its back for a few seconds, its neighbour will copy it moments later. She also found that when the first instar nymphs hatched, they immediately sought out companions. Adults tend to feed together and hang out in clumps when resting and grooming. In the winter, they can amass by the thousands as they find some tree crevice, some old building, some heating duct, some crack in a house as they go into torpor to overwinter. My neighbour, Dawn, remembers the winter of 1969 when, due to a huge seed crop the previous summer, cedar bugs arrived indoors in such numbers that they were piled ten centimetres deep on windowsills. Like people at rock concerts or sporting events, cedar bugs are keen to congregate.

In the *uninterrupted* life cycle of the cedar bug, males and females die after the female lays her eggs in May and June. In the 10 days it takes for the eggs to hatch, the male and female join their ancestors. The crunchy, mummified bugs, like half of those between the panes of glass in front of me, are those who did not survive to mate and reproduce. Though cedar bugs seem able to survive extreme cold, moisture and cold combined can do them in. That, or falling on their backs. It is no surprise that a good portion of the bugs between the window-panes are lying in that familiar, on-their-backs posture, stiff legs in the air. How many of us have watched Geoffrey flail, legs motoring? How many of us have extended a finger to let its tiny but gripping claws take hold so it can flip over? But if Geoffrey is a dead bug if it falls on its back, why does it happen so often?

One rumour has it that cedar bugs are blind. Why else, people reason, would they walk in endless circles and bump into things the way they do? I make a motion to poke into the centre of the windowsill cluster and the six of them bend their knees to shirk my descending finger. Cedar bugs can, in fact, see well and have a highly evolved sense of touch, so blindness, clearly, is not a contributing factor in this behaviour we fail to understand.

Some people suggest that cedar bugs are just excessively stupid. In our modern, I-want-it-yesterday world of high-speed communications, commerce and life, slowness has been equated with a lack of intelligence. If you're slow, you get left behind, that's a message inculcated by our culture. But what is it that we're afraid of being left behind of? If we take our time to cook and eat (heard of the slow food movement?), to muck in the play dough with our children or to sit and observe the natural world, what are we really missing? An episode of a sit-com? An e-mail joke doing the rounds? A moment to be seen, fashionable and ambitious, at yet another event? What if we allowed slow to connote joy, persistence, depth and beauty instead of stupidity?

Besides, what does stupid mean in light of the fact that insects are the most successful of the animal groups? From an ecological perspective, insect life is a marvel. I have only to spend a few minutes watching a moth wave its fantastically feathered sensory antennae or marvel at a pair of blue darners locked together in mating skip across the surface of a pond to know that diversity in insect physiology, behaviour and habitat are unparalleled in any other animal group. Insects live on land, in the air, in water and make up 75 percent of currently known species on Earth. Billions of them live in every hectare of forest. What we see represents only a small portion of this enormous biomass; some are microscopic while others live hidden away in the soil, in plants, in animal bodies.

Like the six cedar bugs on the windowsill, many insects have the aura of ancient creatures, precisely because they've found a secure evolutionary groove and thus have had little need to change. Given fossil records, it's entirely possible the cedar bug hasn't significantly evolved in a long, long time. Many insects are similar, if not identical today to what they were 40 million years ago. So, if change itself and not the ability to change, is our measure of smartness, then cedar bugs are stupid. But if survival and perfection in adaptability are the goal, the species is a genius.

Western Red Cedar

elp

Cedar bugs have figured out that sucking on the sugar-rich juices of conifer needles in the fall will help them produce or synthesize the anti-freeze that will enable them to survive the freezing temperatures of northern winters. Their proboscis, though designed to pierce conifer cones and seeds to suck up the food therein, has been put to work on over 30 species of trees including the pistachio. Indoors, one neighbour spotted one sucking on a jade plant. Their complex salivary glands, which secrete an enzyme rich saliva, and allow them to dissolve and suck up the solid material in seeds, are an evolutionary coup as well. In terms of opportunism, cedar bugs have excelled in recognizing a good place to live in the human constructed boxes that have only recently arrived in their homeplace. And when it comes to the ability of the cedar bug to expand its range, we have to give it nothing less than a prize. Before 1920, *Leptoglossus occidentalis (Heidemann)* was an exclusively western species. By 2000, it had established itself in many places in Eastern North America, having caught rides on travelling Christmas trees, in apple boxes and other human-propelled devices.

Behind me, the guest turns the pages of his book, the cedar bug long forgotten, while I stare out past the cedar bugs at the ever-fattening snowflakes and the occasional clump of snow descending in a slushy whump from the roof. I catch myself wondering how well cedar bugs did before humans arrived on the scene with our tidy shelters. I also puzzle over the fact that Gale Ridge-O'Connor found that the majority of cedar bugs who congregated indoors were male (our male name for them thus suitably chosen). She theorizes this may be due to the relatively larger size of the female, but do we really build houses with cracks so precise as to let in Geoffrey but preclude Mirabelle? It's not that the females are absent, just not so present. After all, the sight of cedar bugs mating is not unfamiliar.

The male initiates the copulation by approaching the females from the left side, tapping the female's head and antennae with his antennae. If she doesn't want him, she boots him away with her hind leg, using the leaf-shaped tibia like a club. If he's an okay dude, he gets to telescope out his abdomen and run his genital capsule medial notch (there isn't a penis, don't bother looking for one) over her paraproct lobes until she opens them up and lets him in. The actual mating act can take anywhere from 3 minutes to 24 hours. They usually begin in the evening, so if you find two cedar bugs locked together during the day, they're the ones giving it the full run for their money. If they move during this time, it's the female who waddles, pulling the male along behind her. Once they're done, they each look for a new partner, preferably someone experienced. Apparently, cedar bugs have a bias against virgins. Go figure.

The female then lays (actually oviposits) her tiny barrel shaped eggs on needles or leaves *outside*. As far as anyone knows, they don't lay their eggs indoors because there is no food for them. By the time they hatch, their parents are just husks of their former selves. This usually occurs in late spring, thus beginning a new, but yearly, life cycle. The hatching takes 10 to 21 days depending on numerous factors that biologists are only beginning to explore. The newly hatched nymph, or first instar, is orange with an up-pointed abdomen that makes it look like a tree bud. Though residents of the Columbia Mountains have seen adult cedar bugs in numbers, most of us wouldn't be able to identify it in the first few instar stages.

In the end, scientists know very little about *Leptoglossus occidentalis*. It seems no one has examined their unusual flying technique beyond noting that cedar bugs are strong flyers. Apart from a few wasps which parasitized Gale Ridge-O'Connor's laboratory subjects in the North American east, little has been published about what preys on cedar bugs. Mostly, scientists have concerned themselves with how to control *Leptoglossus occidentalis* which, being the opportunistic species that it is, has found an excellent source of food in the nursery seed groves of British Columbia and elsewhere. Like many other insects, the cedar bug is primarily of interest to researchers if its activities have a negative impact on human lives and our human economies.

Yet, we ignore the insect world at our peril. While some are gnawing away at our commercially valuable crops or biting our furless backs, many more are making our lives possible. Entomologist Gilbert Waldbauer asserts that less than two percent of insect species make life difficult for humans. The majority of them — the grotesque, the scary, the beautiful, the recyclers, the pollinators, the food chain anchors — make our survival possible. As pollinators alone, they keep food in our larders and flowers in our gardens. In the Columbia Mountains, cedar bugs help keep northern flickers, black-capped chickadees, Steller's jays, pileated woodpeckers and other birds adequately fed through the winter. In pursuit of cedar bugs, woodpeckers and flickers have been known to peck holes in people's houses, making a considerable racket and a nuisance of themselves in the process. The cedar bug is clearly a crucial link in the food chain, making this part of the Earth the place we know. Given our extraordinary dependence on them, our fear and dislike of insects is downright strange, if not outright self-destructive.

I put my finger out and one of the six Geoffreys on the windowsill accepts my invitation and climbs step by slow step on board. The grip of its tiny claws on my skin registers as only a tickle. It backs away nervously as I lift it up to eye level. Its antennae dance in front of the brown spots of its eyes. Geoffrey has watched me sleep, eat, make love, read books, dance, sing and everything else I do to occupy my winters indoors. And here it is, living, eating, breathing, mating and dying at my side. What untold, undiscovered stories — its and others — are waiting, waiting for each of us to uncover?

The Hieroglyphics of Extinction

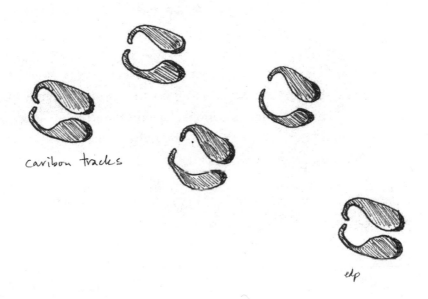

caribou tracks

elp

Eileen

In my first few years here, I resisted spending very much time outside in the coldest months. Like the winter light, I retreated when the days shortened and the shadows lengthened. From a safe, warm house, I measured the weak rays of sun as they dribbled over the rim of the mountains. I waited for the golden orb to return. It never occurred to me that I might still find the sun, if I looked hard enough outside. Eventually, though, like an animal foraging for food, I learned that if the sun couldn't easily find me in winter months, I had to be prepared to seek it out. I began to ski and to snowshoe, finding my way to the tops of ridges or to sunny places in the valleys, following those well-lit patches in search of brightness. Once I was in the habit of being outside, I noticed that not long after the winter solstice on December 21, something magical happens. The sun begins to rise on its arc again. This process becomes most noticeable in February. By this time, winter begins to feel as if it is over, even though some of the coldest, snowiest weather is yet to come. Rays of sun flood back into the valleys, illuminating every snow crystal and sharpening the graceful reach of bare limbs. Unobstructed by deciduous leaves, unabsorbed by lush, green growth, the light bounces and dances across the dormant landscape.

On one such diamond-studded day in February, I stepped my boots into my battered cross-country skis and headed up the Clearwater Creek valley. Clearwater Creek drains into the Salmo River. The valley it flows through ascends gently toward the subalpine. As I began my steady climb up the trail, I notice that the ski tracks were deeply grooved and icy after almost two weeks without fresh snow. Shreds of arboreal lichen littered the trail. Animal tracks everywhere recorded busy movement. I noticed tracks of a snowshoe hare, just to the right on a sloped bank. I saw tiny marks — made by claws or feet — and these were followed by a long, shallow swish. What had made this unique combination? A bird with tail feathers? A small rodent whose tail swept the snow?

Hunter-gatherer cultures once studied animal tracks carefully. These tracks were the landscape's written messages, hieroglyphics etched in the ground or pressed in the snow. Hunters could "track" an animal by following the depressions. I saw some more tracks further off the trail, these much larger, broad and shaped like a shallow teacup. They emerged from a fringe of white birch, cedar and hemlock. They might have escaped my notice were it not for the fierce light casting each track with a vivid blue glaze, perfectly defining the outline of the animal's foot. These tracks were too large for deer, too clean for cougar. I leaned sideways on my skis, trying to get a closer look. Could they be from caribou?

The hooves of caribou are nearly round and well out of proportion for the animal's size. Scientific theories suggest that caribou evolved large hooves as an adaptation to the snowy landscapes they frequent. In the Columbia Mountains, the hooves act like snowshoes, giving the animals winter access to tree lichen draped over the middle and upper branches of mature conifers. As the snow accumulates, the caribou gain access to lichen higher up the tree, an important winter food for the animal.

Most of the caribou in B.C. and the Yukon — those of the "boreal" or "northern" variety, range back and forth across open landscapes, searching out sedges or ground lichen. As the glaciers shifted and shrank following the last ice age, the caribou living in these mountains adapted themselves to the more vertical climate and geography, an accomplishment that has earned them their own sub-species term, "mountain ecotype." They learned to forage from valley bottom to higher ground. They found food seasonally, nibbling wetland sedges, horsetails and grasses in the warmer months, false box and tree lichen in winter.

I stood in my tracks, contemplating my next move. For caribou, roaming across their home is an act of survival. For my culture, survival seems to be connected to keeping within safe bounds. My life overflows with examples of how I limit myself, how I define my concept of place tightly. The house where I live sits on a lot with sharply defined edges. Though the land has no fence, an invisible barrier marks its perimeter. So, too, the border between the U.S. and Canada draws its political line through towering mountain ranges and rushing rivers, severing connections that are natural to the landscape. I wonder sometimes if the modern human attraction to boundaries signals a rejection of the deep-seated willingness to roam. Trapped between white lines, behind fences and even inside cars, it's not easy for us to respond to the roaming instincts we all have within us. Way back when, all of us were hunters and gatherers, those who roamed the landscape opportunistically in search of food.

I would need to step out of my skis to get a closer look at those tracks. Did I want to sink into snow up to my hips? I wore only two layers of cotton tights. Not having a wide set of hooves, I felt my desire to see the tracks clearly fade more quickly than the light on a winter afternoon. Here it was again, my resistance to roaming, especially into deep, untracked powder. I began to rationalize the decision to stay where I was. I didn't know enough to identify the marks for certain anyway. What difference would being a bit closer make? Further to that, what did it matter if caribou had been through this valley or not?

A Sinixt hunter would have risked the deep powder. He would have been prepared from late childhood by his father and uncles to recognize all sorts of tracks, to read them and learn from them about animal movements. The tracks would have told him where to find the animal and when or how it might best be taken as food. The hunter would have worn clothing of tanned caribou hide and carried snowshoes crafted of woven maple saplings for just such a situation, snowshoes like those the botanist David Douglas traded for in a Sinixt village when he stopped near Nakusp in 1827 on the way up the Columbia River. The family lodge where he stopped, Douglas said in his journals, contained "not fewer than a hundred" caribou skins. Yes, a Sinixt hunter would have known instantly if the tracks I had seen were those of a caribou.

I moved on, skiing steadily up the gentle incline. The sun had begun to slip lower in the sky and I knew I would need to move quickly to make the round trip to the patch of old growth forest near the end of the trail and then back again, all before dark. But as I climbed, the image of the tracks followed me, tugging at my curiosity. With it came a developing sense in my mind that the caribou might very well have passed through this forest recently. To share a forest track with caribou wouldn't sound all that remarkable in other areas of rural B.C. where large herds of the animal still survive. But here, in a valley of the Columbia Mountains, the sight of a caribou or even the sight of a caribou's tracks would be remarkable. While the populations of deer and elk have stabilized or swelled in the past several decades, the numbers of caribou have faltered. At the turn of the twentieth century and again from mid-century until now, the estimated population has declined and then declined again.

Of the five remaining herds, only two measured in triple digits at the start of the second millennium. The other three contain 41 or fewer animals. One of those dwindling herds has been hanging out for the last several years at the height of the Nelson Range in the Selkirk Mountains, on the eastern side of the Salmo River valley, far above the valley where I ski. According to provincial government biologists, this small herd and the other two in the South Purcell and Monashee Ranges are at very high risk for extirpation, meaning the loss of a species in one specific ecosystem. If current land use decisions contribute to the destruction of all the herds here, then the mountain ecotype caribou specially adapted to these mountains may no longer exist in B.C.

I moved to the Columbia Mountains in the mid-'90s, halfway through the most precipitous, 10-year measured decline of the species around the province. While a decline in numbers appears to be the consistent story of the caribou over the past century, the years between 1990 and 2000, were, according to the scientists, particularly bad ones. Historical accounts such as Douglas's indicate that the animal was once a keystone of the Columbia Mountains ecosystem. In the past decade in particular, caribou have become more and more of an abstraction. They seem to exist in idea more than in reality.

I have never seen a caribou in the wild. I know what they look like only because I have seen photos or paintings. They are like moose in the lumbering thickness of their shoulders, like deer in size. Their compact, muscular bodies are adapted for migrations, during which they can trot for hours. They have wide nostrils with special valves to close off breathing, to avoid inhaling insects, or to limit the intake of cold air or water. Their eyes are the colour of winter creek water, dark and expressive. Their soft, wide lips are specially adapted for nibbling vegetation. They wear a muff across their shoulders and sport a wide branch of antlers. In Europe, they are called reindeer. In Canada, they go by *caribou,* related to a French-Canadian word, *carribeouf.*

In the autumn long ago, when caribou arrived in the valleys to harvest wetland sedges and participate in the annual rut before snow began to fall, the Sinixt would drive them into the rivers, killing them from canoes. In winter, male caribou lingering in the valley bottom would have been taken individually, with bow and arrow. Pregnant females moved up to the alpine where they would sequester to give birth when weather warmed. Caribou, sexually mature within a year or two and having a life-span of seven years, could have flourished with persistent but respectful levels of hunting. All they needed was a place to call home, a habitat to serve their needs.

Once Sinixt hunters had successfully stalked a caribou, the animal would become the product of the whole village. The culture frowned upon hunters taking personal credit for a successful kill, and upon hording or waste. The women tanned and fashioned hides into clothing, shoes or blankets. The people ate meat fresh or pounded and dried into jerky. They pulverized bones for marrow and polished horns for handles or utensils. All parts of the caribou found use. The animal became a part of the people, and they a part of it. Herds ranged numerously along the wetland fringes of the waterways and in the deeper, darker forests, offering a steady, predictable supply of nourishment and warmth.

The most significant winter food for the caribou is the black tree lichen, also known colloquially as witches' hair. A better local term for this might be Coyote's hair. The Sinixt have a legend of the lichen and how it came to the landscape as food for their survival as well as that of the caribou. One day, when Coyote tried to capture two swans, they carried him high into the air. They let him go without warning, and as he fell, he lodged in the branches of the trees. When he freed himself, some of his hair stayed behind, hanging from the limbs. This hair he transformed into _skwelíp_. It was a staple food for the people, especially in times of scarcity. The Sinixt pit-cooked the hair-like fibres of the lichen and pressed them into cakes, making food with the consistency and colour of black licorice.

I reached the old growth section of the trail, thinking about Coyote hair and survival as I skied into the trees where large limbs dripped with the black hair. Here, a shred of the original caribou habitat survives in a forest of gentle spaces rising from deep snow. In more than one way, the survival of the people connected directly with the survival of the caribou herds. When a Sinixt hunter grasped a handle made of polished caribou antler, when a Sinixt woman pounded the caribou flesh with a stone pestle and then dried it in on a hot slab of rock beside the fire, when a child was given a first pair of moccasins stitched from the animal's hide, they must have felt a direct gratitude for the caribou's presence in their land. Here was the gift of home, being passed through the animal to them in a bond of place, animal and culture. That bond would have been felt deeply, as a form of love that can only be imagined today.

In terms of developing any sort of modern relationship with the caribou, it seems that imagination must play a role, given the animal's shrinking presence. American conservationist Wendell Berry speaks of the role imagining can play in conservation. "If we are to protect the world's multitude of places and creatures," he says, "then we must know them not just conceptually, but imaginatively as well. They must be pictured in the mind and in memory."

Historical accounts of the caribou are landmarks for deeper meaning that can be cultivated through the imagination. They are suggestions in which the soul might take root. During the summer of 1859, John Sullivan, a member of Palliser's expedition, was helping to forge a trail over the Summit Creek pass near the U.S.-Canada border, up in the Nelson Range, where the caribou now congregate much of the year. At the height of land, Sullivan came across what he thought was an "Indian trail" to help the expedition find its way. But he had been mistaken. His native guide told him that in fact it was a "carriboeuf road." Caribou, he was told, roamed the mountains and valleys in large number. "The woods are traversed," he wrote in a report, "by their beaten tracks."

The woods are traversed, I muttered to myself as I felt the tips of a hemlock branch brush against my shoulder, *by their beaten tracks.* It is easy to conjure the image of expansive herds, countless numbers of "carribeouf" finding their way through the high mountains and forested valleys of the Columbia Mountains. *By their beaten tracks.* These four words, a typeset footprint, a hieroglyphic of the landscape, continued to echo in my mind. How many caribou might there have been in these mountains, to create *beaten tracks* in the dense, nearly intractable wilderness Palliser explored? Were the caribou, our own region's version of the plains buffalo, once too numerous to count?

If environmentalists keen to protect the caribou could have their way, all logging of mature forests in core caribou habitat would be halted immediately to save the animal from extirpation. If the logging industry could have its way, all cutting practices would continue at their current levels and the caribou would have to do its best to survive in a forest of clear-cuts that research strongly suggests does not suit the animal's biological needs. At a local conference exploring the future of the mountain caribou in the Columbia Mountains (sponsored in 2002 by the Columbia Mountains Institute of Applied Ecology), some biologists emphasized many factors other than habitat loss in the declining numbers: predators, disruption from winter recreation, fragmentation from road construction and certain cut-block procedures. Snowmobilers at the same conference claimed that their sport can co-exist with the caribou herds. The one topic not openly or thoroughly discussed was the rate of logging in core caribou habitat areas, or the impact of that logging on the animal's survival. The mountain caribou appears caught as it is between ecological idealism — attempts to save the caribou from extirpation — and the economic reality our culture has created — logging practices that strive for efficiency and high levels of monetary profit.

As an observer of the debate, I recognize that the values of our society, values that favour fences and enterprise over tree lichen and the freedom to roam, may not shift in time to save the caribou. As a culture, we may not have the ability to live in a home that is wild, undivided, and less managed, a home that would have natural appeal to the mountain caribou. This undivided sort of home, where forests have the time to mature, where they can spread and lengthen

93

across a space large enough for a wandering animal, this is the kind of place the mountain ecotype caribou needs to thrive.

The light began to fade as I skied further through the mature trees. Here the shadows were no longer blue but almost black. Historical surveys describe high levels of hunting by settlers early in the twentieth century. This was the first known threat to the animal's survival, though numbers appear to have recovered at least partially by the 1950s. Once industrial logging began to build roads and harvest with speed and efficiency after about 1970, a different sort of exploitation began, that of caribou habitat, rather than of the animal itself. The destruction of habitat has had a far more permanent effect on the size and strength of the herds. Homes are a necessary element for survival. The fragmentation of the caribou home has restricted the ancient movements of the animal, removing large portions of its food supply and challenging its ability to use the landscape in the way it has always known.

The mountain ecotype caribou is "red-listed" by the B.C. Conservation Data Centre, which means that in British Columbia, it is threatened or endangered. The caribou's continued decline suggests that for some reason, it is not protected well enough by forestry guidelines on the use of Crown land in Canada. The animal is not protected at all on private land. And while it has been protected by stringent legislation in the U.S. for some time under the Endangered Species Act, that protection ends abruptly when the animal ranges back across the border to search out food on the Canadian side of the Selkirk Mountains. Only recently has the caribou come under the protection of the Species at Risk Act.

"People *exploit* what they have merely concluded to be of value," says Berry, "but they *defend* what they love." The mature trees seemed to be reaching toward me with their arms, enclosing my

94

human form in their arboreal shadows. An old growth forest holds a weight and a drama that does not exist in younger forests. It speaks with a sonorous voice, one informed by the cycling of many seasons over time. I skied past several mature hemlocks, their feathered branches draping toward the ground. The shaggy bark of the cedar almost glowed in the approach of darkness. The light had grown too dim for me to search for more caribou tracks here. Perhaps it was the mood, the developing darkness, but I decided that it didn't matter if my sighting of caribou tracks was an act of imagination. As I skied hard to turn back onto the main trail and began the long coast back down the trail out of the valley, I questioned in my own mind whether the culture I am part of might be able to love an animal we barely know, a forest we have barely walked in. If Wendell Berry is right, if we wish the caribou to flourish in this region, we may need to shift our experience of the landscape and its wild creatures from mere value to love, from scientific knowledge to passion.

Protecting places for animals when their needs conflict with our own requires a justification beyond economics. The culture may choose one day to preserve large tracts of forestland for caribou, or to dramatically alter forest practices to create or maintain more mature forest stands. To do so would provide increased habitat, and maybe even something else. Wild, sparsely peopled places can also have an effect on a sense of inner freedom, on the ability to *feel* for the truth of landscape intuitively rather than prove its existence in a tightly bound, rational space.

Stepping out of my skis, I decided I would return to the old growth woods I had just been through when the weather was warm, when the sun had melted the snow, and when I could wander freely as the caribou once did in the Columbia Mountains. I would drift among the lichen-crusted trees, unimpeded by skis or even snowshoes. I might even take off my shoes to rub my own soft pair of hooves against moss on the forest floor. I wanted to feel for the caribou's presence in mature woodland, to search out its unique hieroglyphics of freedom as they imprint themselves historically on the land. I wanted to understand what it means to roam.

In my kitchen the next day, I talked on the phone to a scientist involved in research on the caribou. As the logging industry clears the forest around them, many of the few remaining animals have been fixed with radio collars so that scientists can track their movements. They are being carefully watched for their ability to survive the consistent loss of habitat. How much of their home can disappear without them being lost altogether? When I tentatively told the researcher about seeing tracks in the valley bottom, he didn't laugh out loud or tell me I was crazy, as I had anticipated he might. "That's entirely possible," he said. "Some of the herd has moved. Radio signals have been picked up across the valley from where you were, in the Bonnington Range."

The caribou might very well have crossed the valley along the Clearwater drainage where I had skied. Perhaps I could call the blue-glazed tracks a true hieroglyphic after all, a symbol with scientific as well as imagined meanings. The caribou lumber quietly and almost unseen along a path littered by our region's industrial use of wild, natural spaces. Ranging in a time-honoured way for food, herds cross through more and more clear-cuts. They migrate into flooded valley-bottoms only to find the wetland grasses and sedges gone, replaced by reservoir silt. The females climb to calve on steep subalpine slopes clear-cut in patchwork fashion, exposing them to increased numbers of predators who stalk them by hiding at the edges of clear-cut patches. The interior mountain terrain of the Columbia River watershed seems vast, but it may not any longer be large enough to be home to the caribou and human beings, both. The caribou may be too old and too wild to live in the confined future we are shaping for the landscape.

Hieroglyphics have many layers of meaning. Could the track also express the fact that the caribou is finding its own way to survive here, even in drastically reduced and barely sustainable numbers? Scientific evidence suggests that the herd congregating in the Nelson Range and moving across to the Bonnington Range appear to be stable, fluctuating around 35 to just over 40 animals. The stability of this herd could demonstrate that it has found a way to live in the forests we have created. This strikes me as near to a miracle: that the animal could maintain its roaming, herding ways despite all the interruptions to its freedom.

Hieroglyphics are enigmatic. They are not anchored in the rational mind, like an alphabet. They have the ability to represent single words, whole concepts, complex visions, important truths. They tell stories. Stories of old-growth forests, plentiful herds, polished handles or near-extinction. Stories of what it means to live somewhere a long time, what it means to roam, what it means to imagine and to survive. I may never see a caribou. But nothing can stop me or anyone else from following its tracks toward a boundless home.

The Tree Inside Me

K. Linda

...Silently the birds
Fly through us. O, I who long to grow
I look outside myself, and the tree inside me grows...

Rainer Maria Rilke

December 14, 2002

On the small, three-log bridge over Wren Brook, I pause, as I often
do, to let my eyes adjust to the dim, filtered light of the forest beyond.
Here, in the snowy hollow that cups the stream, a constellation of

cedars, larches and hemlocks typical of the Interior temperate rainforest grow tall and dense. My breath hangs in smoky puffs in the still
air. All is quiet. In the warmer seasons, there is often a wren nearby
to trill me a welcome to these woods but with winter in full stride,
quiet reigns. I step onto the snowy path alongside the glistening
black flow of Wren Brook; the path is only a suggestion, but my body
knows the way.

I walk among the tall larches, the buttressed cedars, the scaly
hemlocks and dying pines, as I often do, seeking solace, stability and
quietude. This is home to me. Like the Sinixt people of this valley, my
Estonian ancestors were once inseparable from their forest home. The
ancient Estonians worshipped the forest — its springs, rocks, animals
and especially its trees — for thousands of years. Whether wise or
simply enduring, trees seem to embody a power, both symbolic and
literal, that few humans can deny. Trees thrive through rootedness.
They move with wind and snow. They re-create themselves in fertile
abundance, occasionally grow very large and unimaginably old, and
provide for many other beings. For me, the forest is not an element of
place, but place itself, complete and infinite. From its intricate body, I
can gather all that I need: warmth, food, medicine, water, light, inspiration and peace.

It is all too easy for me to get lost in reverence for the forest. So
much so that I tend to forget the challenges the forest can offer up.
Forest fires, for example, are a natural and semi-regular occurrence in
these woods. With climate change and our interruption of natural fire
cycles, serious forest fires are an increasing threat. Much as I have
tried, I cannot imagine how I would tread this Earth if a wildfire
ripped through the Bird Creek valley and left but charred poles of
these tall trees I am walking among. A fire, natural or not, would
change everything, me included.

I stop and place my palms against the furry bark of a tremendous cedar. Where its roots stretch, red-skinned, out from under the edge of the snow into the stream is an evergreen leaf of wild ginger, a reminder of a different, more abundant season. Fire doesn't need to rip through this forest to show us its ability to transform; the forest's wealth endlessly translates itself each and every year. Worms and bacteria manufacture soil, mycorrhizae and roots within the soil carry its nutrients and water to trees and plants. The greenery, in turn, absorbs sunlight and air, in turn, feeding the abundant insects, birds and mammals who also eat each other. Eventually, all the parts return to the soil. The loop is continuous. And *these* forests of the Columbia Mountains are particularly active, especially in places like the Incomappleux Valley, the Duncan River and the Westfall, all just north of here.

Temperate rainforests are among the most biologically productive ecosystems in the world and this swath of forest, running from central British Columbia down into the northeastern United States, is unique. As an Interior temperate rainforest, it hosts both coastal as well as drier ecotypes and species, thus providing home for a stunning diversity of life. In terms of trees alone, the Interior rainforest contains more species of trees than anywhere else in British Columbia. I have only to wander the Bird Creek valley to discover 17 species, everything from subalpine fir to western hemlock to ponderosa pine. Whereas a tropical rainforest might host a few hundred species of mycorrhizae, the subterranean fungal threads that lace the soil, temperate rainforests can have thousands, joining the forest up in a vibrant network below the ground.

The air tastes clear and watery with a tinge of evergreen as I continue up the path. In the summer, the air sings with the fragrance of the devil's club that grows lush and tangled along the brook's edge while the fungi, bacteria and rich soil play base notes of this symphony. The snow muffles the water notes, the bird notes, the wind notes and my foot notes, muting the symphony, creating a sense of shelter. Even the filtered light speaks of an interior space. Only the white pines, dead from blister rust, admit light. I gaze up at one tall, pale, woodpecker-pocked column of wood that transmits ribbons of sunlight down to the forest floor where sheets of its ash-grey bark are heaped. I walk on.

As I continue up the gentle incline toward the place where the trail dips precipitously down to Bird Creek, I puzzle over how many people in modern societies think of forest as a mere collection of trees. Though there can be no forest, in a long-term sense, without trees, these towers that surround me are just one element in a complex web of life. Rock and rich soil are its underpinnings and water is its blood. When timber companies talk of "forest health" they actually mean the non-rotted wood of the trees that represents a marketable commodity. When they talk of reforestation through planting trees, they speak simply of an impossibility. How do you plant a lichen, a squirrel, a springtail, a creek? How do you re-create the natural processes of water, of nutrient cycling, of soil stability, *of wholeness* once these have been interrupted by logging?

Interruption. I scramble down the slippery slope to the creek. There, a line of concrete and steel holds water against the mossy banks to provide for our domestic and electricity needs. When our land co-op constructed this micro-hydro installation, we joined the electrical era in a unique way. We realized the dream of many a Columbia Mountain dweller by acquiring our electricity "off the grid." With the creek at its winter low, I skip from rock to rock below the damsite with ease. On the other side, I set off along the vague trail where our pipeline runs. Not 20 metres from the weir, I stop dead in my tracks. There, above our hydroelectric pipeline, hang strips of flagging tape — neon yellow, pink and orange.

The flags wave at me like a red blanket before a bull. They represent a dramatic change in my forest home that is neither desirable nor natural. A change that is of the magnitude of a forest fire, but is the work of people: industrial logging. In the face of this change, the forest asks something new of me: it asks me to be a warrior.

Almost six years ago, a local sawmill informed us of their plans to log the forest of our home watershed, Bird Creek. In the austere, fire hall meeting room, the company's head forester spread out maps for the watershed committee members to examine. With great self-assurance, he laid out the company's five year logging plan in terms I scarcely grasped. Twenty percent of the forest would be cut. Clearcuts and some "partial cuts." I didn't know what to say, what to ask. *What did you expect?* A voice inside me wanted to know. We of the tree-rich Columbia Mountains are well aware of what sway the timber industry holds over public lands. I struggled to explain to the company what was at stake for me.

At home, I grieved the news. I picked up my pen and wrote about my love for forest. In the calm of the following morning, I reread what I had written and realized that I felt called to do more than simply express myself. The forest had given me so much — how could I refuse this call to arms? By noon, I was on my way to town to photocopy my treatise. I distributed this wad of eight pages to 50 friends and acquaintances, close to home as well as across the continent and overseas. That was the beginning of *The Drum*, which I have published four times a year ever since.

As I ponder the gaudy flagging tape, the sign that the logging has arrived at our doorstep, my stomach knots up. The very act of speaking out for the integrity of the forest has robbed me of some of its solace.

Like a tree that loses its top to lightning or wind, I have to search for a new way to grow.

December 24

My land partners, Joe, Jessie, Christopher, and I make a trip up to the logging site close to our land today. We cross the icy creek at the big landslide and scramble up the steep slope grasping at trees and roots protruding from the snow. Joe carries wire, staples, KEEP OUT signs and a hammer in her worn out knapsack. As I heave myself upward, I notice that the part of me that lives in wonder of this forest has retreated, curled up in some remote corner of my psyche. I no longer seem to know how to live in my love of this forest except to muster up my most ardent defense of it.

We arrive at a sturdy Douglas fir encircled by two bands of blood-red flagging tape. A third tape, a gaudy barber-shop-striped one, warns us that this tree is to be used as an anchor for the logging cable that would haul trees up the slope. This will kill the tree. The problem with using this particular tree is that it is on our property, not Crown land. Crown land is, in simple terms, public land but as a group of the so-called "public," we've had only spotty success in asserting how we'd like to see this land used.

My blood boils as I stand in front of the flagged fir, stunned by the gall of whoever marked this tree. For the six years I've been involved in the watershed committee attempting to alter the course of the prospective logging in Bird Creek, my land partners and I have consistently spoken out against industrial style "rape and run" forestry. For them to mark a tree on our property for use in this destruction implies one of three things:

1. that this violation of private property happens all the time and because they get away with it, they keep on doing it, or

2. that industry feels it has a moral right to all land, and the rest of us are just inconvenient squatters, or

3. that industry does not wonder if anyone would object to helping out with the use of an expendable tree, or

4. that somebody made a mistake.

Faced with flagging tape on *our* tree, my land partners and I set to work. We tack one KEEP OUT sign to the Douglas fir itself and add in marker, "This is our tree; you cannot use it" to the sign. I hug the tree fiercely before joining the others to tack signs along the boundary of our land and string wire at this location as well. The Crown side of the land has no obviously suitable tree to anchor the cable, we note. The live trees here are not very mature and there are many snags (dead standing trees) especially the towering, old white pines. I gaze at all these trees, live and dead alike, knowing I will not be able to prevent them from being cut. For a moment, my defenses fall and, standing among them, a wave of shame passes through me. Isn't there something more I can do?

I push the question and my shame aside. Christopher, Joe and I decide to continue along the blue flagged property line to check out the second proposed cutblock on our boundary.

In the past, I have relished these adventures to the far reaches of this land we claim as "ours." There are no roads, no paths, only the tangle of forest, whose understorey opens up periodically where clumps of big trees shadow the ground. But today, as we trudge, my heart is heavy. Even though we remark on the specially large or beautiful trees — a puzzle-barked ponderosa pine, a dimpled-green aspen — my new found mantra plagues me: What next, what else can we do? As we scramble back homeward, we agree to strategize among ourselves over the next few days. Meanwhile, we listen for the tell-tale signs of the logging coming closer, the roar of machinery, the whine of chainsaws, the crack of falling trees.

January 6, 2003

I wake up from a dream with my heart in my throat. In the dream, I'm on a campus where there is much coming and going. I'm standing in a parking lot looking at someone who is up a tree. I go inside a building where a young Native woman is waiting for someone to talk to about going to school. A fellow comes along and tells her she can combine architecture and movement and build stainless steel monuments.

As I contemplate my dream, I realize how strong the pull is to intellectualize the impending forest destruction above. The person up the tree is abandoned for talk about stainless steel monuments. What does the person up the tree think of this? She is the part of me that does not want to be reasonable. Other logging I have fought with a principled, intellectual and compassionate approach, the way someone defends someone else's rights. These trees, however, fall into the sphere of my immediate home. For them, I have passion, rage and love, but I do not know how to translate this great welling of emotion into the protection of my home forest.

I see that it's not realistic or even appropriate to vent all my pent-up anger about the disrespect of the Earth on this one situation. Even so, as I climb out of bed, my body vibrates with it. I keep reminding myself that what is being done here is relatively minor, just a small nick in the much larger swath industry cuts through what I value. The forest will recover in its own way from this pillage. And I will get some rest from this long wait for the company's arrival at this point. The wait will finally be over in under a month, leaving behind wounds that will eventually heal. The circle of rationalizations my mind conjures up do little to calm the panic the dream induced.

Scars will remain. What do I need to do, after the loggers have gone, to heal the fracture I see growing inside of me? I'd like to do something in those cutblocks but what? A ritual? A removing of flagging tape? Or before. There is still time to mark each tree with some touch of love. I wonder if the injecting of dyes into trees has been explored? Pink wood, green wood, orange wood — what would the sawmill do with that? *Think brain, think!* I plead as I pad down the stairs to eat breakfast. But no, my old friend, the brain will not help me out this time. Something else is called for now. Maybe it is the way of the warrior to abandon reason.

January 10

Today, Christopher and I go up the mountain to meet the loggers.

The men and their machines are at work when we park the truck and cautiously approach the widened spot on the snowy road. A strapping, shaven Doukhobor man (of the pacifist, anti-materialist sect of Russians who settled this area in the early twentieth century) in a neon orange jacket approaches us, a determined smile ready on his face.

"Hi."

"Hi. You must be Kay," he begins.

"K.Linda. Yes. We live below." I gesture awkwardly at Chris who introduces himself. We shake hands. He mentions that the company's logging supervisor had been up that morning, bringing them up to date on our concerns. He says they will be walking our pipeline and property line with the supervisor before any work gets underway. He gestures to the logging at hand, a relatively small clearing where a chainsaw buzzes and trees continue to fall as we speak. He talks about how they are leaving lots of so-called "wildlife trees", and about how narrow they've made the cable yarding corridors. Around us, the fat trunks of cedar and douglas fir are piled up well over my height.

"What are they doing with the cedar?" I ask.

"Telephone poles."

So that's where the forest is going. This thought almost sends me into a tizzy but part of me fails to be provoked. What use of these trees would I be happy with? Wasteful paper use? Panabode houses for wealthy Japanese? Dimensional lumber to madly consuming North Americans?

Since I became involved in forestry politics, I have seen far too much logging, clear-cuts and big tearing machinery to be startled. A certain numbness walks with me through my days now. Over the past five and a half years, some part of me has come to accept that this act would occur. I have also, during that time, viewed industrial logging from many angles, enough to know that what the guys are doing here represents one of the lightest touches conventional industry knows how to make. I am not surprised when the contractor gestures at the small clearing (under one hectare) and says, "We're doing a really good job here. Don't spend any time worrying."

I know he is not lying. His shining blue eyes seem to suggest an honest, warm man who, in his world, attempts to walk in step with his beliefs. He's a working class, rural tradesperson who takes pride in his work. Because of this, he is not afraid of us, or hostile. I appreciate this but only give him a nod, not a smile. If I am a warrior, is he the enemy?

Christopher and I wander up the road to a cutblock that was logged in December, where a driveway width swath leads to a small snowy clearing. I am distracted by the trees that continue to crash to the ground behind us. A cedar, another one, another one. We wander back to the landing and wait for the faller to come up. It's quitting time and these fellows are as eager as the next working stiff to go home to their warm houses. The faller, a lean red-headed chap emerges with a chainsaw and three empty chain oil jugs. The majority of that oil is now on the ground, in the snow. Will I be drinking it in the spring?

Christopher and I walk away. The crew drives away. We all go down the snowy road to our respective homes. As we drive back to our houses, I watch the telephone and electrical poles flash by. I remind myself to say a thanks to the forest next time I spend time on the phone, for it pays dearly for our cherished lines of human communication.

January 27

Chain-sawing and machinery rumble very close now. I am listening to Egyptian musician Hamza el Din and his strangely calming music in my study. While meditating by the creek this morning, I couldn't hear the chainsaws due to the gush of the creek. Unseasonable rains and snow melt have made it louder than usual for this time of year, but every now and then, the Earth moved, a deep echo in the soil and rock itself, probably from trees falling not too far up above. Even while meditating, my heart raced. I asked myself not to be anxious, not to be afraid, but I am. I am afraid of the confrontations we'll have with these men when we go up to stand our ground. I am afraid of the power they have.

Last night, my land partner Jessie and I talked about the world we face in our collective future. I described the feeling I often have of watching events unfold through my half-spread fingers, like a child at a horror movie who is afraid but doesn't want to miss anything either. On rare days, I think of the future as some adventure where I'll bounce through the events somewhat invincibly, trusting, like Jamie Lee Curtis or Xena, that I'll come out the other end unscathed, unaffected. I wonder what it would be like to feel so fearless — or oblivious — every day?

Just last week, I attended a conference on the local effects of climate change which laid out what has already occurred in our ecosystems and what is likely to come. What is to come, is not clear. Devastating fires of unnatural intensity? Losses of species? Unprecedented floods? Rampant skin cancer? How much can we tamper with our own, ultimately fragile, lives?

January 29

Joe and I have now spent two full days up in the forest next to the cutblock. By the time we arrived yesterday, half of the block had been cut already, creating an opening in the woods. Wandering into the block, we find trunks of all sizes strewn every which way, a pick-up-sticks of trees that, only that very morning, were still vibrant, living beings. Fresh sawdust splotches the snow. We sit at the edge of the forest with our backs to the block. Though we are there, we would much rather be elsewhere. We pour tea from our thermos and huddle over our steaming cups for something else to focus on as much as to keep warm.

We sit like this for a few hours, cold and unhappy, until we begin to question what we are doing here, and if we should stay. Just then, Joe's dog Sheba spots a lone figure picking his way down toward us. In his orange hard hat, it is the wiry, red-headed faller Christopher and I met the other day. We tell him about two trees whose tips have been felled onto our property. As we walk over to look at this almost stupidly minor infraction, we explain to him what we are doing there. My unrehearsed speech about the six years we have sat through watershed committee meetings and received little consideration comes out in a gush.

I tell him the only place we have left to defend is our own property and yet this whole valley is our home and the source of our water, power and lives. I tell him we do not hold him responsible, but rather the government and the company who allow irresponsible planning and logging to occur. I shake inside as I speak but my words come out clear and strong.

He listens attentively. We tell him we intend to stand on our own property and that we trust he will not cut any trees that may put us at risk.

He agrees with this and asks, almost rhetorically, "And I can count on you to stay behind that line?" We nod. For the men who work on the ground, our presence is a safety concern. His profession is surrounded by stringent safety regulations set in place to keep it from being, as it once was, the most dangerous job in the province. He sets to work on the rest of the block, eyeing the trees he must carefully, but persistently, cut. Joe and I take turns sitting on a mossy stump, watching him work. Soon, the chainsaw is roaring and the trees begin to fall, one after the other, big and live, big and dead as well as every small one in between. I wince for the small ones in particular because they will not be used. They are cut simply because they are in the way of someone's vision of the ideal tree plantation that will replace this forest.

As he works away at the opposite edge of the cutblock from us, I notice a very tall, glorious white pine near his cutting. Oh no, I think, not the pine. The forest dweller unfurls from a corner of my psyche to focus on the one pine. There are so few of these trees surviving; the ones who have resisted the blister rust are the only hope of white pines regenerating and persisting in this forest. Not the pine, I plead silently, and rise to my feet. I consider traversing the block, interrupting him, speaking out for the life of that particular tree but I do not go. I watch as trees fall dead to the ground wondering how I will approach him safely, how I will make myself heard above the racket of the chainsaw. Heart pounding, I step into the cutblock. But as I

111

head toward him, he begins to move upslope, leaving the big pine standing. From my new vantage point, I see from the flagging tape that the pine lives just outside the boundary. It feels impossible to hold each tree in my heart like this. Surely it will break.

A sound imprints itself in my psyche. It is the strangely unnatural whine, the high airy whistle of a healthy tree, full of green needles, boughs and branches, picking up speed as it falls to the Earth with no forest to slow or interrupt its trajectory. The whine is punctuated by the heavy thud of trunk and crackling of branches breaking. The boom echoes in both the narrow valley as well as deep in the Earth. The faller wears protective earmuffs, but I am certain he feels the trunk's impact through the soles of his feet. For each tree that falls, I struggle for a second to catch my breath.

January 30

We encounter the faller again this morning, this time accompanied by the contractor and the logging supervisor from the company. Again, Joe and I explain what we are doing "on site."

The contractor is clearly distressed by our ongoing presence. The faller is nonplused, and the supervisor decides to argue with us. "Just what do you hope to accomplish here? This logging is a done deal. You're not going to stop it."

We repeat our spiel from the day before, fending off his interruptions. They cannot deny our right to stand here even if they think it is stupid.

In a moment of exasperation, the supervisor looks me in the eyes and says, "I love your passion." Stunned, I say nothing in response. Perhaps I should tell him that love and passion are all I have to go on at the moment, since he and his company hold the power to change the course of events.

I go off with the contractor and supervisor to look at potential problems and violations caused by their activities, leaving Joe to monitor the tree felling. After the contractor treks back up to his work on the logging landing, the supervisor tells me the story of how he tried, for years, to get a job with this particular company because they were the most progressive operation around. "Other places, you only go in and strip the Earth. They don't take any care." He tells me the story of the unionization and de-unionization of the mill a few years ago. He occasionally makes statements about what he thinks I think, what he thinks I would do in this or that situation. Though we have a companionable afternoon together, it is clear that he has pigeon-holed me. He asks nothing about my life, my ideas, about my passion that earlier he claimed to love. He thinks it more important that I understand his motivations than that he understand mine. If he is guilty of nothing, why all this effort to defend himself?

January 31

Since yesterday afternoon, we've been spending time with the fellow who deals with the cables they use for hauling the cut trees out of the forest. He's a different character, very talkative and friendly. He bucks up some dry white pine so we can have a campfire to keep warm. He tells us that he's heard from the faller that we got a bum deal from the company. Interesting and good, I think, that one logger should understand our story in this way and communicate it to another.

I spend part of the day reading a report on a neighbouring watershed and potential restoration and rehabilitation projects in the area. I simply cannot sit here watching tree after tree thud to the Earth.

I realize that these years of fighting for the integrity of my forest home has transformed me into more than just a warrior. I have stopped asking what the world has to give to me; instead, I ask, what do I have to offer the world? How can I be part of creating a community where all people are adequately cared for, where Earth systems are respected fully, and that in living good lives we don't use more than our fair share?

February 28

This morning, instead of sitting down to write, I hike up to the damsite. I realize that I'm resisting everything but sleep these days. The level of anxiety in my body makes concentrating on anything, even knitting, difficult. Already, the snow is shrinking and the small black snake of Wren Brook has begun to swell. Walking through my cherished forest calms me, but something is still amiss.

The logging is not over but the clanging of the machines recedes as it rounds the curve of the mountain. The noise is now a backdrop for the birdsong that has exploded this week. For a whole month, I have been avoiding the cutblocks. I cannot look at the hole this experience has left inside of me. I recall Rilke's line, "O, I who long to grow, I look outside of myself." Since I'm at the damsite already, I decide to trudge up the slope to the nearby cutblock.

I climb the piles of criss-crossed trunks that line the edge of the forest and emerge into the cutblock. The snow is almost invisible among the profusion of abandoned trees and strewn limbs. I shake my head at the waste. All of the dead standing pines, which provided glorious homes to cavity-dwelling birds and animals, have been felled and left to rot. Though these "wildlife trees" have been deemed too low-quality for the mill's needs, they were sacrificed nevertheless in the name of regulations or because they were considered "decadent growth." I even saw the friendly faller go out of his way, out of the marked cutblock, to cut down dead or dying white pines. Like the

114

Sinixt who relied on these trees to build their canoes, they've been deemed irrelevant to the future of this place. Like the salmon that no longer swim these rivers. Like the caribou whose numbers dwindle on the edge of extirpation.

The only sign of new activity in the mess of the cutblock are the piles of cone debris that have formed on the fat trunks of the abandoned white pines. The squirrels have been at work. This is where the squirrels' food was stored even if they've had to move their nest. A robin coasts through the empty space, glad for the disturbed soil that offers up insects and their larvae more easily. Now begins a similar yet different process of forest. Growth is inevitable, but the question remains: what will grow here?

I contemplate the scene. Soon, the company will arrive with tree plugs of certain desirable timber species, with their roots soaked in fungicides and pesticides with names like Cymbush, Rovral and Benlate, and insert them into the Earth. An attempt will be made to repel parts of the rainforest that are not marketable timber — like the fungi, the insects, the unfavourable tree species. Still, I am convinced of the forest's ability to fully re-inhabit these small patches. In time.

In the meantime, the natural kingdoms will interact with this place differently. Ecologist Jane Claire Dirks-Edmunds described both the sudden and gradual transformation of a forest logged and then left to regenerate. Twenty years after the logging, she wrote, "Nearly 60 percent of the insects we had found in the mature forest were no longer there. Also, I discovered that . . . many species and entire families from the young forest had never before been found (there)." Similarly, the plants and fungi were different and different birds and mammals used the area. It is, however, precisely these beings who move between old and new forests that guarantee its perpetuation. It is through the digestive systems that soil bacteria, fungal spores and seeds pass intact, ready to re-establish themselves when the conditions are right."

Unlike the Dirks-Edmunds study area, no roads or skid trails were punched into the blocks in lower Bird Creek. The soil has been left relatively undisturbed and is, hence, more open to new growth, less prone to erosion and landslides. Unlike on the cement-hard roads where heavy machines have left impermeable scars, here the soil is still open to receive. The ground is, after all, where it all begins.

When I climb back over the mound of fallen trees into the older forest from the recently cut one, I cannot help but put my trust in the land's ability to heal these wounds. If pessimism and optimism are both possible choices, someone once pointed out, why not choose to be an optimist? It is true that the land remains. And though my body remembers the terrible whine of live trees falling, the horrible thump of their impact, I too remain. I must trust that time will fulfill its own agenda within me. I will rediscover Rilke's "sublime and moving spaces." I will continue to be a forest warrior. Like an old tree with a broken top, I need only time and the season's first rains to grow a glorious, forked top.

Snake Day Tribute

K. Linda

Today, March 17th, is the Estonian pre-Christian holiday of *Ussi-paev*, Snake Day. If I had a home or house snake, this is the day I would set out scraps of meat for it to eat. If my house snake didn't appear in my kitchen, I would leave my offering next to the manure pile by a barn we don't have. Martin and I would greet our house snake with joy, glad to see it again after the long winter and we would introduce all those who live in the house to it so that henceforth it could recognize its own people. It would dwell through the warm season with us, keeping other snakes, as well as rodent populations, at bay. In its lustrous body would coil our promise of luck, health, fruitfulness and wealth.

Though the sun beams in the window by my desk, there isn't much chance I'll be seeing any snakes today. It's likely the local snakes are still curled in twisted balls in their hibernacula beneath the layers of snow that still cover the forest floor. At best, the gleeful birds, whose morning choruses grace my visits outside to pee, will show themselves to me: golden-crowned kinglet, dark-eyed junco, pine siskin, black-capped chickadee, Stellar's jay, common flicker. It should be Bird Day instead! But no, the ancients celebrated that over a week ago to mark not the arrival of birds, but the turning of their beaks northward from the lands of deserts and jungles. I picture some of my summertime companions — warblers, for example — flitting about lush tropical forests downing a last few mouthfuls of beetle larvae or fruit before setting out on their arduous journey north.

For Snake Day, I decide to send two greeting cards made of my homemade paper, one to a friend in Estonia, the other to my friend Karen Warkentin, a long time student and lover of the snake and now a professor of herpetology. As I rummage for the snakiest of my cards I can find — perhaps next time I make paper I could include snakeskin instead of a wasp's nest — I muse about my own relationship to the snake.

I did not always have an affinity for reptiles. From childhood, I remember only one encounter with a snake. In a golden sea of late summer grass, on some thin-soiled knoll of the Canadian Shield, I ran with a group of children I did not know very well. They were bigger, older and braver than me. I remember wind, I remember sun, I remember the perfectly rounded "esses" of the small sage-green snake that was held out to me. I clutched my hands to my belly; someone had already taught me to be afraid. Nevertheless, I reached out and grasped the snake. My palms still recall the shocking smoothness and muscular curl unlike anything I had ever experienced. It nipped me and I dropped it. I ran to catch up with the others.

I said not a word to anyone about what had happened, especially not my mother. A snake bit me; what a furor that would evoke, first concern, then accusation. Why did you touch it? Are you stupid? In my memory was the vague outline of an incident at the cottage. One summer day, my mother had peered down from the porch to behold a black snake sprawled on the sand next to where my brother and I were playing, oblivious of its presence. I imagine her pell-mell race down to the beach to snatch us out of the evil creature's reach. Until this day, she recounts the story with a vivid horror, her tone never losing the pitch of terror. Children are not naturally afraid of snakes. They learn their fear, it has been found, primarily from their mothers. My mother undoubtedly experienced a similar terror and warning from her own mother and incorporated it into her knowledge of the world.

Snakes must be the most feared and hated creatures in many places on this planet. The irony of mothers keeping alive and passing on this aversion is that snakes have been powerful symbols of feminine power in many different cultures in many places around the world. Often, snakes were revered as Goddess incarnations. In medieval Europe, even as Christianity was making its inroads, snakeskins were tied around women's bellies to ease birth. In some African tribes, a snake going to a woman's bed is a message from the spirit world that her next child will be born safely. Almost universally, the snake, with its ability to shed its skin and emerge anew, has been seen as a symbol of immortality. The serpent has also been a water deity in many cultures, especially in arid places, and the word "serpent" originates in a Sanskrit word meaning snake or running water.

In colonized, Christianized cultures, no metaphor holds quite the negative heft of the snake. This is, of course, not coincidental. Christian missionaries and European colonists alike, inspired by their hatred for the snake that caused the fall of humans from the Garden of Eden, rained fiery condemnation down on any snake worship they encountered. What had been a symbol of water, goddesses, knowledge, immortality and life, became an Earthly manifestation of Satan. Yet in many cultures that have largely lost a link to their pagan, snake-honouring pasts, information about this past, like the notation of Snake Day on a current Estonian calendar, persists. However, this is but a small step on the road to helping people recognize the value of snakes. North American biologists, Karen tells me, have found that people will go out of their way on roads to run over snakes whereas they ignore frogs and swerve to avoid turtles. Snake: kill it. Kill it with the passion of someone who believes that danger and evil can be stamped out. Kill it.

Ugh. I do not want to think about snake hate and snake death on this beautiful day. Snake Day should be a celebration, I think, if not of individual snakes themselves then of the cycles of renewal and change they signify. If we can learn to overcome our fear of the reviled snake, we are well on our way to overcoming all the Earth-dishonouring beliefs our culture has imbued us with. Then, we can truly set foot on the land road back to being an Earth-loving people. In our densely populated, industrialized world, the presence of snakes, especially poisonous ones, is a sign of a relatively intact ecosystem. Places where snakes persist are places where humans have not torn asunder the food chain. They are the home of either profoundly Earth-honouring people or no people at all. These are places where, like our garden, the land manifests abundance.

I decide to head over to Joe's house for our rendezvous to plant seedlings for our garden. Planting the tomatoes, basil, onions, leeks and bedding plants for our garden is a fairly significant undertaking but now that we've acquired all the short season tomato seeds we need from last weekend's "seed exchange," the time has come to take action. I suit up in my lighter, grubbier spring/fall jacket and slip on rubber boots.

I take the high trail, which goes past the garden, and sink calf-deep every second step in the crackling corn snow. As I slosh across a squishy stretch of saturated soil, I think of the letter *S*. It seems to me that the letter was gifted to the Romans by the snake for their, and our, alphabet. It is no coincidence, I think, that the sound of a snake's hiss was not represented by an angular *K* or architectural *H*. Instead, the letter we add to our words to imply abundance comes from the form of the travelling snake, streaming sinuously across the Earth.

I did not handle a snake again until I was in university. Even back then, my friend Karen was not just a snake admirer but a snake promoter as well. She worked off and on at a nature centre where school groups came by the busload to be exposed to the wonders of the natural world. There, she would lift docile captives out of glass terrariums for children and adults to hold. I had reached my hands out tentatively, trusting her more than I trusted the slithering animal that was coiled around her forearm. It did not bite me. Instead, it twined like a powerful vine around my hand and wrist, travelling from one hand to the next in sequence. Again, I was surprised by its dry smooth skin and the force of its ability to wrap around my limbs. Through this one gesture, Karen taught me how to open a significant door to the endless exploration, the spiralling, that I think of as the process of living in place.

From above the garden, I look down over the treetops onto the glistening blue waters of both the Kootenay River and the Kootenay Canal. Between the two is the spot where my land partners and I go swimming in July and August. Snakes can reliably be found there, peering up at the grassy shore, their bodies well-camouflaged squiggles against the rocky river bottom. The summer I moved to the

Columbia Mountains, I often went swimming. On one such day, when I was experiencing the breathtaking contrast between a hot Kootenay day and the crisp chill of Kootenay Lake, I looked over to see a garter snake swimming alongside me, its black head barely protruding from the silvery water, its body invisible except for the faint eddies its movement caused on the surface. I resolved then and there to find out which snakes live in the region.

Of all the Columbia Mountain snakes, the rubber boa is the one I most wish to encounter. Perhaps I'll get lucky, I think, as I scurry past the snow-shrouded garden to the compost pile.

Boas are an ancient family of snakes who bear evidence of their evolutionary past in the form of large lungs and vestiges of pelvises and hind legs. Though the large and spectacular boa constrictor is the best known of boas, the majority of boas are smaller and often live their lives in the ground. The rubber boa is certainly no Amazonian giant that will squeeze the eyes out of your family dog or swallow your baby whole. In fact, it's usually only a couple of feet long and distinguished by being rounded at both ends. It spends its days hanging out under rocks and its nights burrowing into the holes of small rodents, munching two or three or all of any nestling mice or voles that may be found there. In fact, its oddly blunted tail, which makes it resemble a large olive-brown worm, could have evolved due to the hazards of this diet. Like many mammalian parents, mice and voles will defend their nests, if attacked. The rounded tail of the boa is waved about as a lure, an alternative head, so to speak, to draw the adult mouse's attention away from the snake's more vulnerable head that's busy eating up little mice. Often, the tails of females are highly scarred from the defensive attacks mounted by rodents and other small mammals who aren't predators.

I take a deep breath, make a wish and throw the blue tarp off the left bin. Though our compost has proven to be a good place to encounter snakes, I am not surprised that all I encounter today is a mound of rotting apple cores and vegetable rinds. No rubber boa, no garter snake: this pile is still too cold to attract any warmth-loving reptile. And the rubber boa is particularly fond of heat.

Though I hear of rubber boa sightings in composts across the river, there have been none on our side. This probably has something to do with the boa's preferred habitat of drier places. The east-west running valleys in the Columbia Mountains often have startlingly different ecosystems on their north-facing and south-facing flanks. On our north side, our forest is made up of a dense combination of hemlocks, cedars and larch, queen's cup, wild ginger and pipsissewa, while the south slopes are more open, and the spaces between the pines are strewn with needles and grasses that attract more elk and deer. The boa likes the dry side.

Over here, on the moist side, we have garter snakes. For one whole summer, the largest garter snake I'd ever seen here in the Columbias — or anywhere for that matter — lived on our compost heap. When we pulled back the tarp that covered the pile, there it would be, coiled like shimmering loops of black and red string. The first time I encountered it, I stepped back, startled. It lifted its head warily, tasting the air with a red, two-branched tongue. Its small dark eyes gleamed and when I leaned closer to examine it, the snake tightened the coils of its body as if to gather momentum for a quick exit. I stood as still as I could, my eyes on its, willing it to understand that I had no intention of hurting it. A certain calm descended upon us as we relaxed our tense bodies. Its sparkling eyes held my attention. I noticed how bright its colours were, more vivid than any of the tens of garter snakes I had encountered since I moved to the area. Perhaps this was because it was old, or at least I assumed it was old from its size. When, weeks later, it shed its skin on the ground next to the bin, the dry crackling case of its former body measured 1.2 metres. Our encounter ended when I lifted the tarp to cover the compost again and heard the swish of its body as it uncoiled and departed.

All regular compost-goers shared updates with each other on the state of the snake. "Yep, still there. It was in the left bin this time." Or, "It stuck around for a few seconds and there was another, smaller snake with it." A yelp from the direction of the garden meant that someone new had discovered the snake. I remember Huguette, wild-eyed and hopping from one foot to the other, proclaiming, "Il y a un serpent! Il y a un grand serpent!"

"Of course there is a snake," I assured her calmly as I approached with a quick stride. Though I cared about Huguette's distress, I was more concerned for the snake's life. "It lives here, in the compost. It won't hurt you." She stepped back from me suspiciously, continuing to scan the ground around her.

"Are you sure?"

"Absolutely," I said, mustering the expert conviction of Karen.

By late summer, the snake had grown accustomed to our comings and goings and no longer slithered away when we uncovered the compost pile. After about two weeks, I attempted to stroke it. Though it slid away the first time I tried, it let me caress its scaly, silky body many times after that. I never dared wrap my hands around its red-striped sides to pick it up. That's the closest I've ever come to having a house-snake. And my chances of seeing a rubber boa? Well, they're slight.

I cover up the heap and head down to Joe's. She is already out on the porch, filling black plastic pots with white-flecked soil and sorting through our seeds. "Happy Snake Day!" I call out to her.

A researcher who was studying the rubber boa implanted radio tracking antennae in their body cavities. He found that the snakes hang out either under rocks or in rock piles. Interestingly, they burrow under thicker and thicker rocks as the summer progresses, thus using rock thickness to keep warm or cool depending on the weather. They also tend to like open areas without forest cover. As I drop minuscule basil seeds onto the moist black soil of each pot, I resolve to go rubber boa hunting this summer down by our swimming hole on the Kootenay River. The place fits the bill: dry, rocky with well-spaced trees and lots of snowberry, honeysuckle and ocean spray. I picture the sun baking my bare back as I wander, flipping over rocks like a bear in search of a meal. But what would I do if I found one?

I am still a little afraid of handling snakes. Perhaps this is not just due to remnants of cultural and maternal fear but also a wise gesture of respect. The memory of that small warning nip in the sun-swept grasses remains with me. I still encounter a tremor of panic when I first encounter a big snake, or an unknown snake, or a snake who rattles its tail. But knowledge of the non-aggressive nature of most snakes and, certainly, all our local snakes, reassures me fairly quickly. That's when curiosity, delight and awe take over. Happy Snake Day!

A Rare Night

K. Linda

Primordial ooze. These words conjure up images: a frothing bog, a land verdant with giant ferns, tree-sized horsetails and grasses like plumes of fire. You can hear it growing, the shush-shushing of leaves, the dripping air, the burbling Earth. And yet, the scene is oddly still. Not a being moves or flies. The ooze is old, very, very old. The only life forms are ones that wriggle in the places where water laps black volcanic sand. Occasionally a wriggler surfaces, eyeing the possibilities.

Hey! There's one now, a brave pioneer, pulling itself across the muck with its ever strengthening fins. It forays out to nibble on greenery, gills gaping desperately, then waggles back to the water. A being with an eye for opportunity. An amphibian in the making.

The primordial ooze is long gone from this part of the world but even in the dark, the lushness of the greenery by this creek is evident.

The mist awakens the pungency of cedar and forest decay. I know that fantastical creatures are peering out from the wet places. It is precisely such a creature we are hunting for. My partner, Martin, and I have joined biologist Marc-Andre Beaucher for a night of his salamander census taking. The three of us press through the tangled undergrowth beneath the buttressed cedars: Marc-Andre in the lead, Martin bringing up the rear. The gush of the creek in spring flood drowns any hopes of casual conversation. From time to time, we stop and shout at each other.

"The moss is still too dry," Marc-Andre bellows, his hand illuminated against the thick moss in the circle of his flashlight beam. "They like it much wetter than this."

He is referring to the salamander we are searching for, *Plethodon idahoensis*, the Coeur d'Alene salamander. Its Latin name suggests something old and vaguely dinosaur-like, though Marc-Andre's description begs to differ. Our salamander is under 13 centimetre long and glossy with a pale rusty squiggle down its back. Martin and I eye each other, unconvinced we'll recognize our quarry when we see it. If we see it. The visual complexity of the forest floor in our flashlight beams overwhelms our retinas with its formidable array of twigs, leaves, cedar boughs and other debris, all embossed on thick moss.

Marc-Andre suddenly halts our advance, pointing to a spot in the moss. After a few seconds, I see the animal he is pointing at: a long-toed salamander. It is similar to the Coeur d'Alene, he tells us, except its back markings are a sage green. A few steps farther he finds another. When I cradle it in my hand, I discover its skin is gummier than that of the slippery frogs I'm more used to handling. It sits demurely in my palm but scrambles into the moss as soon as I set it down.

"The long-toed is pretty common," Marc-Andre tells us, "but it's often found in the same places the Coeur d'Alene likes." He has been returning to this creek from time to time to hunt for Coeur d'Alenes even though none have been found here.

Marc-Andre Beaucher is one of a handful of biologists working under the direction of Kimberly-based biologist Penny Ohanjanian, to study the Coeur d'Alene salamander. Penny is the first biologist in the region who turned her attention toward this small and secretive creature and set out to discover both its range in the area and its natural history. In an attempt to protect the salamander's vulnerable niche in the habitat, she also set out to study the threats that it faces. That, in turn, lead to the study Marc-Andre is working on, looking for and monitoring Coeur d'Alenes at other potential sites. Given these salamanders are nocturnal, you could say he's moonlighting on this job. During the day, he's likely to be found in the wetlands at the southern end of Kootenay Lake, not far from the town of Creston, working on another endangered amphibian, the Northern Leopard Frog.

The Coeur d'Alene salamander is "blue-listed" according to the B.C. Conservation Data Centre or "threatened" according to the Committee on the Status of Endangered Wildlife in Canada (COSEWIC). This means it is in danger of becoming locally extinct, or extirpated, from the Interior Rainforest of the Columbia Mountains. The Canadian Species at Risk Act, also known as SARA, which only came into effect in 2003, has been the subject of intense debate. Many conservationists believe the legislation is inadequate because it only applies directly to federal lands such as parks, military lands and jails. For a species such as the Coeur d'Alene salamander, the onus is on the British Columbia provincial government to come up with a recovery plan. Furthermore, there is no mandatory habitat protection and species designations are reliant on political discretion, not hard ecological evidence. This leaves the majority of the 1000 species at risk in the province vulnerable.

However, hard ecological evidence can lend credibility to any campaign and the point of the Coeur d'Alene project is precisely to help conserve this species. When the project began, the Coeur d'Alene salamander was known from only four locations north of the border; now, biologists know of 44 sites and can, as a result, help prevent inadvertent or deliberate destruction of these sites.

Researchers have hypothesized that the Coeur d'Alene in B.C. is a remnant population from a time, 2,000 to 4,000 years ago, when the climate in the Columbia Mountains was cooler and moister. They have survived only in places like this low elevation riparian zone where moisture is abundant and there are deep fissures in the granite for the salamanders to escape freezing in the winter and desiccation during the height of summer's dry heat. The population in British Columbia is at the northern tip of their range which extends south in the Columbia Mountains to the Selway River in Idaho and the Bitterroot River in Montana.

Like many species of animals, Coeur d'Alene populations are most secure in the centre of their range, and most vulnerable at its fringes. Small changes in their habitat can be enough to upset their fragile ecological niche. Like other *Plethodon* salamanders, the Coeur d'Alene breathes through its skin and the lining of its mouth. Like other amphibians, it absorbs moisture through its skin instead of drinking. In order for the skin to remain porous to both oxygen and water, it must be moist.

It must be moist. These words rebound in my thoughts as we continue to pick our way upstream. Everywhere I place my hands on the ground, I come away with the impression that the moisture is only superficial. Though it is raining now, it's been a dry spring, and the ground is far from saturated. Still, we move forward, peering into crevices and at the abundant layers of step moss as we go. The rock walls of the gully rise higher around us until we can advance no farther. "Here," Marc-Andre gestures up at the verdant, vertical rock next to a waterfall, "is just the kind of habitat they like best." Here in the splash zone, the surface of the moss is wet, but when I plunge my fingers into the greenery, I feel that the moisture has not penetrated very deeply. We scan with our lights, our faces upturned. The spray and the misting rain tickle my skin. After a few moments, the roar of the creek enters my bones. The rock walls curl in on me, concentrating the sound, concentrating my awareness. And suddenly, I am no longer inside the sound but it is inside of me as though I am a hollow tunnel for the flow of water. The boundary between what I know as me, and the place where I stand, has evaporated. The feeling is awesome. We stand like this, each of us wrapped in our own experience, for many minutes. When our scanning lights fail to reveal any salamanders, we give up our search.

Though we find no Coeur d'Alene salamanders anywhere along this creek, I am not disappointed. The beautiful night envelopes us as we concentrate on climbing back down over the slick boulders by the creek's edge. "Tell me you like your job Marc-Andre," I shout, sidling up to him. "I love my job," he replies emphatically. Although I would like to hear more, I do not ask him anything else. Like many biologists, he is a person of few words and the place for words is clearly elsewhere.

As we scramble back downstream, the world is still only as large as our flashlight beams, but as we near our vehicles, the swoosh of a passing truck reminds me how close we are to a well-travelled road. In the dark, it is easy to forget that we are not in the middle of pristine wilderness. The highway, which snakes alongside Kootenay Lake, passes farms, summer homes and settlements. Each summer, thousands of recreational vehicles ply this route. Above the highway, logging roads take off here and there to access the once abundant forest. Our small visual field belies the enormous impact of the larger world.

Over the past few decades, herpetologists have sounded the alarm about declining numbers of frogs and other amphibians worldwide. Like canaries in mines, amphibians may foretell of the risks we all run by changing our environment. Although no one clear reason has emerged for the sudden decline in amphibians, increases in ultraviolet radiation (UVB) due to ozone depletion, climate change due to global warming, loss of habitat due to human activities, increased pesticides and herbicides in ground water and the introduction of non-native species are all major suspects in amphibian declines. In recent years, it has become apparent that UVB-tolerant species like the Pacific tree frog continue to thrive.

Where does the Coeur d'Alene salamander fit into this picture? Being nocturnal, it's not likely to get sunburned, so to speak, but climate change in the Interior Rainforest is predicted to set a drying trend that may affect it in the long run. Already, seasonal patterns of precipitation have changed, bringing more precipitation in the winter and less in the summer. Also, more of the winter snow is likely to fall as rain at low elevations. This may have untold impacts on species who rely on seasonal rains for breeding. But, by far the most serious threat to the Interior Rainforest population of Coeur d'Alenes is habitat loss. Tree cover is essential because a canopy of boughs over a creek helps keep soil moist and water cool. Because it lives in and around small streams and seeps, which receive little or no protection under current forestry legislation, its habitat is sometimes destroyed directly. Where riparian areas are protected, the narrow reserves are often insufficient for the needs of the salamander.

Even if their immediate habitat remains unaltered, logging, road building and other development in adjacent areas or upstream can cause water temperature to rise and runoff to increase, a report by Penny Ohanjanian states. These changes, in turn, increase the risk of

132

landslides, bank failures and problematic sedimentation. Soil and debris, swept downstream, may clog the salamanders' rock-crack homes and kill the aquatic insects and larvae that are their main food source. Water diversions bring other risks. Further threats to their habitat, especially where they live adjacent to roads, include the application of road salt, spraying of pesticides, and chemical spills. Also, road maintenance work such as road widening, blasting and the changing of culverts can kill a significant number of salamanders in one fell swoop.

In fact, another serious threat to their survival is habitat isolation. Though the homeplaces of Coeur d'Alenes are naturally dispersed, any additional fragmentation increases the barriers they face for meeting other salamanders and breeding. For example, if the forest were logged or developed between the creek we just left and the next one over, it may become impossible for Coeur d'Alenes here to travel across the terrain to inhabit new creeks or to mate with salamanders who might already be there. As we crash through the line of bush to the road, I ponder what genetic problems associated with inbreeding Coeur d'Alenes might face. Probably not buck teeth.

Next, we drive to a site on another creek where Marc-Andre assures us there is a vibrant population of Coeur d'Alenes. "If we're going to see one anywhere, it'll be here," he tells us. As we get out of our vehicles, he points up at a dry rock face that forms one bank of the road. "I've seen as many as 13 salamanders here on one night. They were on the rock, they were on the ground." He pauses to take a good look. "But there aren't any here now." The ground is bone dry.

"Could the salamanders afford to not emerge at all in a dry year?" I wonder out loud.

"The question is," Marc-Andre corrects me, "do they even need to surface to breed? There's so much we still don't know about the species."

If they do need to surface, I wonder, which is the greater risk: not reproducing or suffering the stresses of heat and desiccation? Since the females only breed every two to three years, a missed year might not be a tragedy. At the same time, since each female lays only six or so eggs at a go, the capacity of the population to rebound from lost breeding seasons may be low. Though how to know? Researchers like Penny Ohanjanian and Marc-Andre don't even know how long Coeur d'Alenes live in the wild. One salamander has lived in captivity for 11 years and is at least that old. But my question underlines a significant problem with conserving species like the Coeur d'Alene salamander in the face of human encroachment. So little research has been done on the species that basic natural history information, upon which to base good decisions, simply isn't available.

From the rock face, we move upstream, single file again. Our destination is closer this time, only a few minutes up a trail to where the stream cascades like a veil from four metres above us. Below the waterfall, a trio of thick cedars grows in among the rivulets. Marc-Andre begins his search among the red roots that grip the stony streambed. Martin and I hunt too. Black beetles, an important source of food for the salamander, scurry from my light. I spot a prehistoric looking dragonfly larvae in the creek itself. On the bank, a long red millipede wiggles among the rocks. I study the undersides of rocks, peer under fallen trees. Eventually, the three of us converge at the base of the misting waterfall.

"There's a nest here," Marc-Andre offers as a consolation prize. He points his flashlight at a mound of clay plastered against the sheer, vertical rock. In its perfectly round opening sits a small bird. A winter wren! It peers out at us, anxious about our proximity. She flies into Martin, bumping off his arm in her attempt to escape this sudden wall of human flesh. Her departure reveals a covey of four tiny wrens with large yellow-lined mouths, but Marc-Andre's exclamation of "There's one!" diverts our attention suddenly and completely. Higher, beyond arm's reach on the rock face, a rusty-coloured squiggle worms away from our flashlight beams. Marc-Andre pops open a plastic container to catch it so that it may be measured and photographed for the census. He finds a twig and begins scraping the salamander out of its refuge. We watch his stick, eager to see the creature up close but anxious that he should not hurt it inadvertently. Having no ears and no voice, our salamander cannot yelp in distress, but I wonder about its panic. Marc-Andre gives up in a few seconds and turns to us to apologize.

My disappointment evaporates. "Don't worry about it," I tell Marc-Andre. "I'm here for the experience. I wouldn't turn down the opportunity to see one up close but it's in no way essential that I do." Marc-Andre smiles. In his work, he takes great pains to leave habitat undisturbed, keeps handling to a minimum, and puts all salamanders back where he finds them. Although he works with rare creatures, I sense that he, like me, is no hunter of rarity. If something is threatened, my inherent tendency is to back away. Perhaps because so many species are endangered precisely through human activity, I have a strong impulse to not add to an animal's problem. This impulse, however, is not a common human impulse.

Ted Antifeau, the Regional Rare and Endangered Species Biologist for the Columbia Mountains, notes that the locations of many red- and blue-listed species are kept secret. "I've had well-meaning people, even naturalists, say we know that such-and-such is around here, we want to see them. The last thing they want to do is harm the animal but this can happen." He tells me that all red- and blue-listed reptile and amphibian breeding sites, as well as bat maternity colonies and hibernacula, are kept secret.

"Even a little bit of disturbance can be critical," he continues. "We're also worried about the illegal pet trade. For example, in San Francisco, there is a rare species of snake that is worth up to $10,000. The rarer the better." In the U.S., amphibians are increasingly popular in the pet trade. Most retail pet stores in North America sell some species of amphibians; the majority of these are collected from the wild. In British Columbia, the Wildlife Act prevents "the killing, collecting or holding captive (of) any amphibian without a permit," but these kinds of regulations are difficult to enforce.

The conservation movement has attempted to foster human protectiveness through high profile public campaigns around specific species. Though public recognition of these species may increase, it is not clear whether the mystique generated by these campaigns actually increases their likelihood of survival. If information about the creeks where the Coeur d'Alene lives rouses people's curiosity to the point where they begin to seek them out, the problems of the salamander may be compounded. Awe and reverence of nature are welcome and necessary, but alone they are not enough. To secure the future of any species threatened by our human activities, our love needs to be accompanied by knowledge of the complexity of an animal's life. First Nations people acquired this knowledge through generations of keen observation and participation in an ecosystem; modern science relies on the intellect through purposeful observation and methods. If we rely only on our intellectual perceptions, or only on reverence, we may fail to reach the essential balance that characterizes the natural world.

As the salamander with the pale orange squiggle on its back wriggles into a rock crevice, its main protection remains its own instinct and insistence on survival. We turn away from the misted rock face and continue our search. After all, we are here to participate in the census that is designed to create a knowledge base from which conservation decisions could be made. I continue my slow motion scan of rock and wood and water's edge buoyed by the visual image, imprinted on my brain from our fleeting glimpse of the salamander, of what I am looking for. I pass over more beetles and other prehistoric-looking aquatic larvae, reminded of how little I really know about this ecosystem. Why is it that I hunt for rare salamanders and can identify a winter wren simply by its song yet struggle to tell the difference between a mayfly nymph and a dragonfly larva? Does it have to do with what I value?

I am reminded of a course in nature interpretation taught at the University of Guelph by Dr. Alan Watson. A few of my friends took this course and each one, in turn, recounted the story of one particular lesson he taught. Somewhere near the beginning of the course, Alan would bring a fragile teacup, a family heirloom, to the lecture and talk about its origins and it significance in his family. He would then leave the cup sitting on his desk as he proceeded to lecture on rare and endangered species. At some point, he would "accidentally" elbow the cup causing it to fall to the floor and shatter. People gasped then sat in silence as Alan gathered up the shards. He would then ask his students to talk about their feelings about the destruction of the cup before telling them it was a cheap thrift store special. Another silence would inevitably follow as anger jumbled with relief, hilarity with puzzlement. Here lay the mind twist: the cup had not changed. Only the students' perceptions of the cup and its value had changed.

The lesson was that how we approach objects, natural or otherwise, and how we value them, is highly coloured by our very human and personal perceptions of their value. His point: that rarity or commonness should not be the basis for our interest or awe in anything. To be a good naturalist and interpreter, one needs to see all aspects of the natural world as profoundly interrelated and of inherent value. However, this is a complex and difficult shift considering that we live in an industrial, consumption-oriented society that prioritizes product over process and promotes material gain as the singular goal worth achieving. "The boy who dies with the most toys, wins," is a popular, local expression. To revalue the interconnection of all beings requires a hard look at ourselves, our lifestyles, our community structures and our culture at large. Shifting our daily realities to match a more integrated worldview may require profound, but worthwhile change. This change will require more than recycling cans and bottles, or walking to work; it will require a transformation in perception. Though this transformation may be harder to implement than legislation and more difficult to measure than population numbers, it does represent a long-term lifeline for the Coeur d'Alene salamander and other animals who find themselves in the predicament of potential extinction. And it is something we can each undertake inside ourselves.

We left the forest that night without seeing another salamander. I may never see the pale orange squiggle of another Coeur d'Alene in my lifetime. But, as I climbed back into the truck for our contemplative night drive home, I felt as if I myself had crawled up out of the primordial ooze and considered the benefits and challenges the land above water had to offer. I recognized the fragile balance that riparian creatures rely on. And as long as there are such places to live — mossy, damp, pungent, undisturbed streams, creeks and seeps where cool air pools and the skin learns to breath — the Coeur d'Alene salamander will survive and possibly even thrive in the Columbia Mountains. After all, it climbed up out of the ooze and inhabited this land with no reverence or help from me.

Ground Truth

Eileen

I accommodate myself to the water, not the water to me.
Lieh Yu-Khou

One winter several years ago, I asked myself where rivers begin. Staring out my studio window into the white stillness of snow piling everywhere, I wanted to know where snow flows once it melts, to perceive what drives snowmelt into a natural channel, to understand how it is that a landscape of opaque, frozen crystals could transform into a trickle, a creek, then a river.

No matter where one travels in the Columbia Mountains, rivers are always nearby. The rocky spires and narrow, U-shaped valleys of this place are ideal for feeding and carrying rivers. Creeks carve rocky paths down the steep sides of the valleys, draining the subalpine and alpine each spring of mounds of snow. The floors of these valleys receive and gather the endless creeks into rivers. Two of the region's mainstem rivers, the Columbia and Kootenay, dominate the drainage system. But there are other, smaller rivers as well: the Incompappleux, the Slocan, the Illecillewaet, the Salmo, the Lardeau. Rivers occasionally feed into lakes, most of them deep and cold. Water here journeys southwest toward the Interior Plateau and eventually to the Pacific Ocean.

When I first felt my curiosity stirring about rivers, I was less concerned with where all the water ended up than with how it began its journey. One day in the late winter of 1999, I sat at my writing desk watching snow fall outside my window. Heavy flakes gathered in the branches of the apple tree. Chickadees arrived, using their wings to clear the snow that had settled on the feeder. The snow should have been melting and disappearing as March drew near, but it continued to pile up. Restless as flowing water, I pushed away from my desk and went out to the Nordic ski area, a place called Apex, named for its location on the high point on the valley floor that hosts the Salmo River. As I plowed through the snow, reflecting on the true path of water, I realized that the braid of creeks flowing among the trails must be connected to the Salmo River. I wondered if the river's origin lay hidden beneath the snow. I crossed bridges over pools that were dark and oily looking. Could these bits of creek be feeding the headwaters of the Salmo? I began to wonder if these creeks could trace me back to the beginning of the river itself, to its headwaters. At this point in the year, I would have trouble searching.

The Salmo used to be known as the Salmon River. It was one of several tributaries in the Columbia Mountains named by settlers for the spawning ocean fish. Old maps mark "Salmon Rivers" in several other locations. Many of the "Salmon River" names have been changed. At some point with the Salmo, the story goes, someone inadvertently dropped the *n* when transcribing the word onto a map. True to its name, the Salmo hasn't had a salmo*n* spawn in it for over 50 years, not since the Grand Coulee Dam blocked the fish from the upper reaches of the Columbia and its tributaries.

The Salmo feeds the Columbia via the Pend d'Oreille River of northeastern Washington. It forms just a small part of the water moving through these Columbia Mountains, but being so close to the town where I live, it is the river I know best. The Salmo is a modest but vital stream, where fly fishing happens, harlequin ducks breed, and dippers flit among occasional rapids. Confined and young, this river's run is brief; its banks are narrow. Within an hour, one can drive the course of it. Perhaps that's why my unscientific mind so easily began to wrap philosophical questions around it late in the winter of 1999. Like a school child's speech, the Salmo's diction was and continues to be more understandable to me than mightier, more articulate rivers like the Colorado, the Mississippi, even our own region's Columbia and Kootenay. Given its marginal flow, the Salmo has escaped the direct effects of hydroelectric projects. In that sense, it is still a "wild" river, a river shouting simply who it is. I like to scrabble here and there on the fringes of the Salmo, searching out plants I don't recognize, picking up stones, thinking about fish. Sometimes, I watch the Salmo's glistening path from the highway, following me on my way south to the U.S.-Canada border crossing at Nelway, Washington. On hot days, I dip gratefully in one of the Salmo's secretive, rock-bound swimming holes. When I stand poised to dive, I see silt sparkling up from two metres deep.

Rivers begin in a variety of ways. Their starting points are usually quiet and unobtrusive. Some rivers trace back to the single, moist thread of a high alpine creek, some burst forth spontaneously from submerged springs in an aquifer, some grow gently from a flat plain of saturated marshes or beaver ponds. Regardless of how they begin, all river headwaters possess that seed-sprouting moment, that creationist twinge, the locus between when something does not exist, and when it does. It is this locus, this place of origin that first drew me toward the Salmo River in the winter of 1998-99.

Several weeks after my ski, the spring solstice arrived. About that time, a vision of a thawed marsh entered my sleep, a seeping place not unlike the wetland near Apex that most locals considered to be the starting point of the Salmo River. I dreamed of cold, brackish water, skunk cabbage sending yellow spears into the spring air, wet tufts of bear grass curving toward the ground. I woke abruptly. Lying on warm, dry sheets, my thoughts rising into the dawn, I began to understand why it had come to matter so much, this quest for a river's origin. I decided that when the marshland near the Salmo thawed completely, I would follow the seeping path to the river's actual beginning. I would find the actual spot, the headwaters of the Salmo River. I didn't know what this spot would look like, or how I would find it. If the landscape was willing to show me the way, I would be able to find it.

The days grew longer and softer. Finally, snow melted away from the valley floor and began to melt higher and higher, until the sub-alpine mountains ringing the valley were nearly bare. A flush of green growth began. I was distracted from my search by spring work in the garden. When I finally did venture out in early June, no snow was visible, not even at the crest of the subalpine ridges, though behind them, in the higher alpine, the melt continued. The spring had been cool and very wet, and the rainwater combined with the melting of record levels of snow meant that the rivers carried water near to their capacity. The West Arm of Kootenay Lake swelled. Talk of a "flood year" began, a year when despite the controlling effects of dams, the rivers might rise to an unsafe level.

I decided to start my search at Apex, the ski area where I had first considered river origins during the winter. Since my ski, I had been asking locals for their opinion about where the river began. The answer I kept getting was that the river began at Apex, near the wetland marsh. One day, with the dogs on bear patrol ahead of me, I followed the bare, scrubby ski trails as they curved along Clearwater Creek. When the stream continued off to the right, I chose the easier way along the cleared ski tracks, almost unrecognizable to me now without their blanket of white. I passed through a grove of mature cedar and crossed over a moss-crusted log skid, which had long ago settled into the damp soil. Indian hellebore opened chartreuse leaves along the vague path. I left the woods and entered a small marsh crowded with floppy skunk cabbages, the chosen springtime snack of bears. My hopes began to rise. This marshy area seemed familiar. As I squelched through a wet bog, I wondered if a beginning can be identified once it has already begun.

A warm, late spring sun beat down, sending waves of cabbage stench up into the air. I could hear water coursing faintly off to my right. I dodged several cup-like depressions in the path. These looked suspiciously like bear tracks, though they had taken on too much water to be recognizable. I stopped to rest on a footbridge where I dried my feet and aired my soggy socks. I took a small magnifier with its own leather case out of my pocket, a gift from a scientist-friend. We had been discussing whether scientific knowledge helped anyone bond closely with landscape. I had my doubts, but he was convinced. This gift was his way of urging me to look more closely, in order to love more. I pulled a few water-worn pebbles from the stream and examined the browns, greys and milky yellows through the wavering glass. Beyond the small bridge and down across the swamp, I saw the stream widen farther, continuing its dance along the valley floor. Though I had no map to confirm my suspicions, I knew somehow, instinctively, that I had missed the headwaters. Things here were looking far too established, too noticeable, too much like a river.

Sitting on the bridge, swinging my feet above the burbling water, I realized that beginnings are not some sort of sudden, slam-bang capitulation into existence. Beginnings are more delicate, maybe even more gradual. Perhaps beginnings are not even definable, should not even be seen. When my socks were nearly dry, I put my shoes and socks back on and began to retrace my steps. It occurred to me that I should stop looking. It occurred to me that I had no right to know, that the precise identification of that source I so keenly wished to locate might not serve me any purpose if found.

I tried again in a few days, and then again, returning home each time with wet shoes, happy dogs and a sheepish sense that — pocket magnifier or not — I was quite ill-equipped to figure out what should have been a fairly straightforward landscape question. I needed help. It was at that point that I fell back on a modern way: I enlisted the support of maps. Answering my question depended on a more intimate knowledge of landscape than I possessed or than my walks had provided me. A map could offer a worthwhile substitute. But I was embarrassed. The need for a map demonstrated how removed from the basic topography of my home place I actually was, how much of a stranger I was to the ground beneath my feet.

At home on my kitchen counter, I spread out a black and white photocopied portion of a topographical map rated 1:20,000 for the area, encircling about 10 kilometres of the landscape where I assumed the headwaters was located. Taking in such a large circle assured me that I would find the river's first moment somewhere between the boundaries. Commonly used by resource management types and serious mountaineers, the 1:20,000 scale maps identify terrain contour lines, year-round waterways such as creeks and rivers, marshland, roads and rails and settlement areas. With the photocopier, I enlarged my map even more, so that I could see each tiny mark it had to offer with greater clarity. If my own slogging through the bush had resulted in no precise answer, seeing every mark that the map had to offer would certainly help me find my way.

I found the thick black line representing the Salmo River on the map, and then traced my finger back up along its path to where it stopped. Picking up a blue pencil, I retraced the line a second time, studying it closely. I coloured over the line as it passed north of the marsh I had been standing in a few days earlier, passed north of Apex and Clearwater creeks, the two feeding streams I had skied over and around the previous winter, then passed farther north still, beyond Rumbottle Creek and some beaver ponds. I paused the pencil in surprise. I had always assumed the beaver ponds were well above the river's beginning. No local I had pestered about the river's headwaters had ever mentioned the possibility that the headwwaters might be north of those ponds, north, even, of the ski area. Continuing with my blue pencil, I found that at least a kilometre north of the most northerly point most locals identified as the headwaters, the map's black line marked "Salmo River" finally came to an end, branching into two unnamed creeks that drained the subalpine ridges on either side of the valley. Here, the map said, in the Y of the anonymous creeks converging on the valley floor after their precipitous drop from high above, the Salmo River begins.

I recalled other words of science. A fluvial geo-morphologist, a scientist highly trained in the dynamics of water flow, had told me a few weeks earlier that the river headwaters would not be at the point of intersection of the two branches of the Y as the map was clearly

145

suggesting, but higher still, at the start of either one of the two creeks up on the subalpine ridge, presumably the higher of the two. I thought about the river beginning in a skyward place out of sight, nearer to the roof of my dreams. The fluvial geo-morphologist obviously had a different belief system than the technician labelling this map. The map indicated that rivers must begin on the valley floor. Creeks can feed a river, the black line appeared to be saying, but they cannot begin it. That is a job for a river, a body of water in love with a valley. Sitting at my kitchen table, dry feet comfortably tucked under my thighs, I became absorbed in the map. Tracing all the other creeks with blue as they curved in to join the Salmo, I then moved north of the abrupt end to the river's line, into an area on the valley floor that had no creek feeding into it from either side. I traced the next pair of creeks north of this area with blue pencil too, and then noticed that they curved not south, as the others had to join the Salmo, but north. The water from these creeks flowed away from the Salmo River, moving eventually to join Cottonwood Lake and then Cottonwood Creek. Suddenly, the answer to the genesis of the Salmo became simple.

Between the south-flowing creeks that fed the river and the north-flowing creeks that fed Cottonwood Lake, the map told me that chunk of land on the valley floor several hundred metres in length might be the place. An abandoned rail line transected it. I coloured this whole piece of land between the creeks yellow. If I could trust the flow of creeks on either side of this spot, if I could trust the map, then I might find the beginning somewhere between them. This location would be what water techs call the *drainage divide*, a point where all water flows either down one side, or down the other, into separate drainage systems, in this case, the Kootenay or the Columbia rivers. Not usually visible with the eye, the drainage divide gives the water a geographic message about which way to go. That point of change

146

on the valley floor, somewhere in the portion of the map I had coloured yellow, might be the genesis of the Salmo River.

Over the next few days, I made phone calls and returned often to my well-creased, colour-coded map. During that time, a flood engineer told me that rivers begin only once they are passing 2.4 cubic metres of water a second, regardless of their depth, width, length or elevation. I now had three different opinions about where rivers begin. The engineer located the start of the Salmo River not high in the alpine as the fluvial geo-morphologist had, not in the Nordic ski area, as locals commonly did, but several kilometres south, way down below even the swimming hole where I picnic in summer. There, he said, the river had become mature enough to be called a "true" river. When I went to the engineer's office with my map to meet him and challenge his view, I referred to my blue lines and yellow zone. He raised his eyebrows at my heavily creased map. Then he conceded that rivers are commonly named back to their point of origin on a valley floor.

"But," he added, "the origin is not necessarily, by definition, what makes a river *a river*." When I asked him about the Salmo's actual genesis, about whether or not it would be possible to identify the landscape's precise instructions to the water at its lowest common denominator, he asked "Why *on Earth* do you want to know?"

From an early age, I have lived with the strong sense that the landscape was not an escape from my humanity, but a place to better understand it. Though I doubted this flood engineer would understand, I knew that the river's headwaters had to do with giving voice to the heart. In the geographic circumstances of this wild stream of snowmelt finding its way through the landscape, I sensed something about the human ability to define the self in a natural way. Originality or authenticity springs not from some arbitrary place along the banks of a stream. It flows from the internal place that makes any of us who we are, from the headwaters of the human spirit.

I left the flood engineer's office confident that I had enough knowledge now to return to the valley of the Salmo River, to walk carefully the ground it flowed across. I wanted to see for myself the drainage divide, this place of significance sending such a strong message to the water, telling it where to go, what to be, how to flow. Given the exceptionally late, record-level runoff from the snow-packed alpine, this might be a good moment in the process to witness such a defining moment. My earlier doubts about whether I would ever find the spot or whether I should continue had been shoved aside. I had been taken over by a compulsion that surprised me with its fierceness. I needed to see the genesis of the river. I needed to see it before high water subsided and the river's original secret seeped below ground again into drier summer weather. There wasn't much time left.

Most maps today are made from satellite or airplane imaging, not by survey work done on the ground. Discrepancies arise between those photographs and the Earth itself. These are usually due to optical distortion or lack of photographic precision. When a precise distinction is required, land technicians seek out what is called the "ground truth," how topography shakes down on the living Earth. I had none of the land tech's equipment: surveyors' measuring devices, hip waders or even a compass. All I had was a photocopied, colour-coded map, my eyes and a compulsion to find the river's origin. That would have to be enough. As a concession to the somewhat scientific aspects of my quest, I decided to take along my pocket magnifier. I set out on my bike near the summer solstice. The year before, the old railroad ties had been lifted, leaving behind a gravel and packed-dirt path. As I entered the abandoned rail line where Cottonwood Creek flows north out of Cottonwood Lake, I took note that the water's flow indeed matched the directional lines on my map: as I headed south, the water headed north, away from me to meet the Kootenay River at my back. Biking farther south, I passed Cottonwood Lake. I heard, but could not see, a creek roaring through the ridge to the west. Again, according to my map, this creek would land on the valley floor and flow north, emptying into Cottonwood Lake, which would feed Cottonwood Creek. I was still moving against the flow of water. As I pedaled, I asked myself whether a valley creates space for a river, or whether the river takes its own? Could the Salmo River read the landscape better than I could read my own heart?

Somewhere within the next kilometre, I hoped to find a sign of moving in concert with the water, of the water going south rather than north, though I did not know what that sign would be. Seasonal streams rushed into the ditch beside the packed dirt road. I smelled the fresh dampness of new growth, of soil soaked with the water of life. I felt excitement and a sense of adventure. I had prepared myself enough by now to know that I was close to something. Farther away, in the tangle of bushes, water formed into small pools and then rushed again into small streams. Each time I came across more water, I peered down at it, checking for the direction of the flow, then I unfolded my map and checked the distance.

I had been pedalling for about two kilometres when I looked ahead to see water overflowing into the path. Could this be it? I pushed hard on the pedals and saw that the water was rushing toward me still, making a rut on the right-hand side, then crossing the road and emptying into a north-flowing creek. Pedalling farther south, I reached a ditch lined with scrub willow, cow parsnip and some grasses. This ditch was being fed by water emerging from a saturated marsh above it, water with an identifiable flow but not confined enough to be called a stream or creek as it oozed down the hill. When the water from the small marsh entered the ditch, it flowed back toward Cottonwood Creek where I had come from.

Something made me stop and get off my bike. I walked 15 metres south down the road and saw that the water was suddenly flowing with my stride rather than against it. How had that happened? Retracing my steps slowly, I peered closely at the water, following it back to its exit into the ditch from the small marsh above. And there, almost indiscernibly, I could see that some of the water was flowing north but some of it was also flowing south, both to my left and to my right, as it emerged from the seasonal marsh overflowing onto the road.

I inched along the ditch until I was standing precisely at the point where I could see water flow both directions. The ripples catching the sunlight glistened in two curves branching away from each other. Snowmelt rippling south (to my left) would become the Salmo River. Snowmelt flowing north (to my right) would become Cottonwood Creek and eventually join the Kootenay River. I could see plainly that the water chose two separate paths.

Of course, locating a place where a seasonal stream parts in two directions does not mean that one has found the drainage divide. I needed to bike farther south, checking all the creeks and water flow until I came close to the ski area, that more extensive marshland where I had tromped several days earlier. Doing this, I could confirm that all the water south of the point I had just discovered indeed consistently flowed south to create the Salmo. Then I could be sure that I had found the river's ground truth.

I travelled the remaining kilometre that I had coloured yellow on the map with some suspense, knowing that at any point I could discover a stream going the other direction. Such a discovery would

150

shatter my developing landscape picture of how the Salmo River begins its dance across the terrain. I stopped at every source of water, even puddles, listening and looking down to determine flow. Eventually I reached the ponds well below the start of the black river line on my carefully studied map. Every single water source I had checked was flowing south to meet the Salmo.

I turned and raced the bike back to the tiny marsh where I had first seen the water form its curving intersection. Kneeling beside the ditch, I fed a few sticks into the flow, watching them turn either left or right, north or south. The bits of twig followed the water's impulse. I knew with increasing certitude that I crouched more or less at the headwaters of the Salmo River. I felt suddenly very small, even in this unobtrusive place. A ditch in a seasonal marsh did not suggest the fanfare or power I would have anticipated for this source. No interpretive maps were posted at the spot. There were no commanding views, no visual feasts.

I recognize the irony of this discovery. The rail line and the ditch that serviced it were both significant human alterations to the landscape that had interrupted the natural seepage patterns of water down the mountain. Without them, the water might have continued on its way quite differently. The ditch allowed me to see the formation of a river precisely. Often, by contrast, a drainage divide unaffected by human development is a dry place, and the scale of a river's genesis is too large to comprehend with any ease — the top of a ridge, the height of a mountain pass. This particular divide might not have been noticed so easily without the destruction. I was learning that I could not plan what I found on this search, that I might not always like what a discovery suggested, that I had to take things as they came. As unromantic as the ditch was, it provided me with a lesson. The dance of my bits of stick continued to draw my attention. I remained in a crouch at the edge of the ditch, thinking about water's complex passages, about the way an origin develops into an existence, and then how an existence, whether it be spirit or matter, follows a path, accretes an experience, becomes something.

From this point, water would flow north into Cottonwood Lake, Cottonwood Creek and, finally, the Kootenay River, winding along a narrow valley and coursing through three dams before reaching the mighty but contorted Columbia River. And, from this same point, water would flow south, seeping through the Apex marshland into the Salmo River, then into the Pend d'Oreille River, wrapping around from a different direction to join the Columbia. After its reconnection with the Columbia River, the water would then bump through dam after dam in the Columbia Gorge, across the great plateau of the northwest, before reaching the Pacific Ocean, several hundred kilometres west of this spot in the Columbia Mountains.

I knew I was standing not only at a drainage divide in a narrow valley along an abandoned rail line at the origin of a minor river called the Salmo, but also as witness to one of the Earth's central landscape functions: the movement of melted snow or rainwater into a welcoming but distant ocean. Like a point on a Gothic arch, this branch of the vast Columbia River watershed begins at a precise point, representing the apex of twin drainage systems that drop with great elegance and complexity from the mountains to the plateau and then to the ocean. Unlike a Gothic arch, this river locus had no pretences, no heavenly aspirations. It was on the ground, placed as such to remind me that authenticity has its source in the Earth, the personal terrain, the place of truth.

Rain began to spit from the scattered, late-spring sky. Bugs were chewing my ankles. I fed my last stick as I thought about the origin of emotional existence, about the passage of people and time through one's life, about those moments of connection that define our presence on this Earth and lead us on journeys whose ends remain unknown. Watching the small twigs move along the gentle wash of current, I realized that origins cannot be discovered through abstract exercises like dreaming or thinking, that rivers cannot be understood by peering at a map. One must feel one's way along the ground, tripping and falling, before learning where the self really lies: here beside this pebble, or there, at the edge of that cliff. In this way, we register the Earth's weight beneath our feet; we begin to discern its truth as ours.

Several years after my discovery, I reflect on the many coincidences that allowed me to see so clearly the origin of the Salmo River. The saturation of the ground from record-setting levels of snow and the late melting of this snow due to a cooler than normal spring may have made 1999 the one in a dozen or more years when I could have successfully witnessed what I did, so easily at the edge of an ordinary ditch. Just a year after that, logging took place along that same stretch of land, upsetting the pattern of flow I had seen so clearly. The opportune circumstances of my search for the headwaters have convinced me that the landscape has its own form of what the Greeks called *kairos:* the soul's own moment, the fullness of time. This moment is the alignment of possibility, the seizing of compulsion, a moment of accumulated insight that makes us finally susceptible to greater understanding. In nature, it is the time when a thunderstorm releases its torrent of rain. It is the sprouting of a seed when it is at last safe to grow. The first frost deep enough to flush the leaves. The gravel nests beneath a kokanee ready to receive the spawn. The moment when a river begins. It is the right time, the right moment, set by a clock whose face we cannot see.

Singing One's Heart Out

K.Linda

Every morning, first thing after I wake, I go to the creek.

Bird Creek is shaded beneath the cedars, hemlocks and cotton-wood trees. The sun reaches into the cool gully mid-morning, spangles the water for some minutes, then angles back out of sight. Sometimes, when I need something other than routine and handiwork, I calculate when the sun is due to touch this wrinkle of the Earth's face and rush here for those moments. This early summer morning, however, I am here for the daily ritual of seeking some peace within me. Since I often have troubled dreams, in which the legacy of my parents' refugee

155

experience haunts me, this ritual is more than just good form. The equilibrium my meditation practice offers me has been a way of meeting my terrors. It is as essential to my survival as food. What I am beginning to learn now is, though peace is a worthy goal in and of itself, it is also a doorway to much more.

I gather my round board from the base of the fat cottonwood that grows on the bank and put it on the three strategically placed stones by the water's edge. I sit down. I scan the slopes and trees to locate myself and any other sentient beings who might be in the vicinity. I take my glasses off and pocket them assiduously to avoid losing them (as I did one pair many years ago). I close my eyes. I meditate.

I hear the creek burbling past my feet. I attempt to empty my mind of all thoughts. I identify the lingering tremors and aches of my body and let them go. I empty my pockets of mundane details and worries and let them swirl away with the water. I take deep breaths of the clear air. I let the feathery summer warmth sift down from the treetops into my flesh. I empty my mind of *all* thoughts and arrive in this place. Then, and only then, does the bird sing its long trilling, silver-threaded tune. It pauses, then sings again, a tune so distinctive and complex, I cannot imitate it despite the fact that these birds have been singing for me every spring and summer for years. A winter wren! A winter wren!

I open my eyes and rummage for my glasses. Tiny and brown, the wren can be hard to spot when he's not singing. He spends much of his time hopping among the fallen trees, leafy bushes and mossy rocks that line the creek gully hunting for spiders, insects and their larvae. To sing, however, he finds a perch and broadcasts. I spot him on the opposite bank atop the unearthed roots of a hemlock that fell across the creek, belting out his song. At 90 decibels, his aria renders him visible, so voluminous compared to his small, round egg-like body with a stubby upright tail and tiny head. He's so close, I can see his thin, slightly curved beak parted in song.

Though I sometimes let him sing without needing to see him, I never ignore him. His song hints at a celebration of life that is beyond survival, beyond contentment, even beyond happiness. His song is a story of such abundant exuberance that I cannot resist its pull.

I love the winter wren. I love this wren for the same reason I love the colour orange. The colour orange, ant-festooned peonies and ample, fleshy women who revel in their fat bodies. They break my heart. They break my heart open.

The Winter wren is small and plain, which is how I often feel. This has been its mode of survival: to blend in, to not stand apart. My ancestors also spent nearly 800 years of colonization and enslavement perfecting this mode of survival. Estonian people internalized the necessity of not drawing attention to oneself. We guard our thoughts, our sorrows, our rage, and even our glee, close to our hearts. Even after the cats have visibly departed, we still scurry like mice, shrouding our truest selves. Rare is the Estonian who dresses flamboyantly or takes on a visible public role. I, like them, live in the underbrush of the great forest world, working insistently, quietly, diligently. Sometimes, I am too Estonian for my own liking.

The gush of the creek recedes as I walk from deep green into sun-lit emerald. People are drawn to animals, especially birds, who represent some hidden or undeveloped part of themselves. The wren, for all its vulnerability, nevertheless takes the space it needs to express the tremendous heart of song that wells up from its tiny body. Undaunted by potential predators — hawks, owls and weasels — when it comes time to sing, it does. Estonian independence in 1991 was the culmination what was called a "singing revolution," great gatherings of people singing in spite of Soviet intimidation.

The winter wren is neither large, nor flamboyant, nor rare. In fact, it is found all across North America, in Europe and in eastern Asia. Yet, for many, wherever it is found, it is a notable bird. Shakespeare's Lady McDuff lamented her husband's departure in MacBeth by noting that,

the wren, the most diminutive of birds, will fight,

her young ones in the nest, against the owl,

all is the fear and nothing is the love where the flight

so runs against all reason.

Though its spunk is prodigious, this trait is not primarily what the wee wren is known for. When I conducted an informal survey of favourite local birds, two friends also cited their fondness for the same bird. Peter is a former tree-planter and a musician. "I love the way it sings," he tells me. With our mutual love of music, we've been enchanted not by the fierceness and relatively ordinary chittering of the female but by the male's unrelenting, exuberant song.

Dave, a geologist, often finds himself in the wren's forest habitat and has had close up encounters with the bird similar to mine. Nicknamed "the tree-planters bird," the winter wren seems to have a penchant for hanging around when people are at work in the forest. As we slog through a workday, the wren reminds us to look up and take note of the beauty of the moment.

In the fall, when mating season is over and the young have fledged, wrens will come close to humans, surprisingly unafraid. I remember a wren I encountered in Glade Creek when I was doing some fieldwork there. The small bird flitted around me within arm's reach, cocking its head this way and that to examine me. I crouched down, equally curious about this bird, whose brown feathers glowed like warm earth in the rich autumn sunlight. Enchanted, I reached out my hand to see if it would alight there, but it only kept on hopping and looking. When I spoke, as softly and sweetly as I knew how, it paused and cocked its head to one side, its eyes bright and shiny upon me. And then it flew away.

Many biologists espouse strictly evolutionary explanations for animal behaviour: each behaviour has a practical function either in keeping an animal alive and fit or in perpetuating its genes. In a Darwinian world, competition is everything. And though Darwinism and Creationism have entrenched themselves by duking it out in certain U.S. schools, some scientists have begun to formulate ideas that incorporate both the scientifically quantifiable evolutionary approach with a larger philosophical, even spiritual, view of the Earth's functioning. They argue that it is time to shift our understanding of the natural world, not to supplant theories such as evolution, but to add new patterns of knowledge to existing facts. Ironclad principles are being re-examined in light of questions that have not been answered by models of survival of the fittest, natural selection, random genetic mutations and competition for resources.

So does the song of the wren make sense in evolutionary terms? What sense could it make for a bird who has evolved to be so small and unobtrusive to fill up the creek gully with his song, to render himself so divinely visible?

Certainly, like other songbirds, the winter wren trills its fantastic tunes in part to establish territory and attract mates. Male wrens tend to be highly polygamous, attracting as many females as they can to the stretch of creek they have claimed. Each spring, between bouts of singing, they busily gather moss and twigs, disappearing into the low shrubbery and downed wood on the banks of the creek to build display nests. At this time of year, their arias announce the tours they give to prospective mates. Males who have secured areas with many good nesting sites are able to build many nests and are more likely to attract more females. It seems the girls are in it for the nice pad, not the fancy stereo. Male tail length, which at best is short, has also been correlated with mating success.

What part of the wren's song is sheer exuberance and what part serves a function? Why do wrens sing the way they do? Researchers have struggled to establish a clear relationship between mating success and the intricacies of wren song. We can retrace our steps, however, from the nice nests to good habitat to territory that was set in place by song, to hypothesize that wren Pavarottis might have an edge. But volume seems to give more weight to this explanation than complexity of song. Male winter wrens often perch on a high log or bush to broadcast their distinctively loud songs which carry for tens of metres even over the roar of spring creeks. So why not just belt out one note like the varied thrush? Wouldn't it make more sense to cut the arias short and get on with building more tidy, attractive nests? If life were only about survival, wouldn't this be the evolutionarily sound thing to do?

These questions, I discover, have lured more than a few researchers into the forest, loaded down with sensitive microphones, parabolic reflectors and reel-to-reel tape recorders. It's hard to think of a more delightful kind of field work than plunking myself down on a lush, forested stream bank and simply waiting for the birds to sing. I envy researcher Beatrice Van Horne who spent two summers recording — and listening to — 6,436 songs of 25 individual winter wrens. I do not, however, envy the work that followed. Digitized and analyzed, broken down into sonograms, equations, charts and tables, the songs were scientifically assessed for the variations of the western winter wren's song.

I learn that whereas eastern North American winter wrens sing an average of two song types and Japanese wrens, six to seven, individual western birds can warble up to 47 song types! *Troglodytes troglodytes pacificus*, who dwells in the Columbia Mountains, has a larger and more complex repertoire than his counterparts anywhere else. Something in these dense, damp, inland mountain rainforests inspires the wren to sing and sing and sing so magnificently. Van Horne discovered that not all wrens were equally inspired and thus the average number of song types for western wrens was 21. *Song types* are any songs that share the first 15 syllables. Given that the average western wren song contains 37 syllables and that she discovered 436 unique syllables in the thousands of songs analyzed, this leaves much room for variation. And vary they do.

After reading about Beatrice's research, I lose sight of the question of why wrens sing so exuberantly and get caught up in the scientific "how's" and "why's." For weeks and weeks, I sit and listen to the wren sing morning after morning, struggling to hear, to follow, the precise melody of the song. Like water, the tune flows and burbles, slipping away before I can grab hold of it. What I do hear is the high pitch, the speed at which each note is uttered, held for but a fraction of a second, before the next one reaches its upturned bill. Sometimes, the wren's song sounds like a 33 LP played at 45 speed. There are melodic bits and more than a few trilling sections. Beyond that, all I can really comprehend is that songs last five to 10 seconds and, after a brief pause, another begins. The wren can sing for hours on end.

Wrens form awareness of one another based on their songs. Wrens in an area share songs, borrowing from others' repertoires, modifying them and passing them on. Though the winter wren's repertoire changes continuously, Van Horne discovered that the songs all draw from a set number of syllable types that are arranged according to discernible patterns. Certain syllables are common song openers, the intro so to speak, while others, like repeated trills, are more likely to be found later in the song. Songs tend to branch at preferred points where new or borrowed sequences are inserted. Some syllable types commonly follow other types, whereas certain transitions are consistently avoided by the singing wren. The structuring of songs was found to follow these rules over time, from season to season, from year to year.

Wrens are thus able to distinguish newcomers in the forest from neighbours based on their songs. If those crafty biologists were to come along and play neighbours' songs outside of neighbours' territories, resident wrens would hurry to check it out. Hey! He's not supposed to be over there! So although the wren is largely solitary, he lives in an auditory community. Does a wren, I'd like to know, become irritated, as some people do, if a song is sung wrong, the lyrics or sequence muddled? Do some wrens prefer some styles over others, creating the equivalent of classical wrens and jazz wrens, pop wrens and hip hop wrens? Audio experimentalists? Metal heads? Are there songs that travel quickly throughout the Columbia Mountains until every second wren has the same tune stuck in his head for a few weeks? A wren aesthetic implies an artistic awareness, which is shared by a community. And culture is what binds a community together.

So often, we human beings have bound ourselves together through our suffering, not through our joy. We have sought those who can understand our pain, in part because we have identified ourselves so strongly with that pain. In these groupings, we have anchored ourselves in the notion of safety. To step outside those groups and risk the adventure of seeking joy is perceived sometimes as a betrayal, sometimes as putting our allies in deep danger. There is comfort in the known, even if it holds us back from possibility.

But can't exuberance be a known too, part of the intricacy of life, and not just a step out onto a weak, high limb? Wren songs, as complex as they may be, are not pure improvisation, a willy-nilly of notes bubbling up at random. Winter wrens have discovered the careful balance between picking tunes out of the air and letting them ride and the small, plain brown necessity of survival. Their music, like their lives, has an internal logic, a structure that informs the progression of a possibility. The wren's song changes with the season. It may alter according to whether there is a potential mate or a potential rival in the area. When attracting a mate, the song has a fantastic internal variety whereas when incubation and nesting are in full swing, it becomes simpler.

But this does not alter the fact that while singing, the bird is not hunting or eating, he is not building nests, he's not giving tours to prospective mates. And, thus, the singing is at what Darwinists call "a high evolutionary cost." "None of the theories of the evolution of this complexity seems to provide a compelling general explanation, either for acoustic plumes or for vocabularies," researcher R. Haven Wiley admits. James Lovelock's Gaia Hypothesis, on the other hand, accounts for non-functional behaviour by recognizing the value of diversity. It is seen not only as the variety of life that exists but also the variety that exists within a species — socially, sexually, physically or otherwise — making both the parts and the whole more stable and resilient. The bird might not sing because he is happy, as the old saying goes, but is happy because he sings.

Stan Rowe, a wise ecologist and philosopher who lived in the Columbia Mountains, wrote: "Professional biologists make no concessions to beauty. . . . The reasons are hard-headed. *Control* of phenomena, not *sensitivity* to them, is the goal of science. Scientists search for mechanisms within, not aesthetic emanations without." He suggests that by looking into an organism or thing, we can find out *how* it functions but in order to find out *why* it functions in the way it does, we must look outside of it, at a far larger picture, one that may incorporate immeasurable elements such as beauty. Lovelock believes that the sum of all living and nonliving matter forms a single self-regulating entity of the planet Earth, and that cooperation, abundance and beauty are elements of natural diversity as much as is competition.

Why is it then, morning after morning, as I plod to and from the creek, that I still need to convince myself that the Earth is truly not a place of scarcity but of brilliant excess? Why is it that the "wee wren, the most diminutive of birds," can sing its heart out while I struggle to locate and express my own voice, my own exuberance?

Our cultures are part of what make us who we are and yet, sometimes those very same cultures cease to serve us. As I let the knowledge implicit in the wren's song enter me, I catch myself in full evolutionary stride. Yes, the world still has its ogres, perhaps more so than ever before, but I am no longer an Estonian serf anticipating the next violation by my German master, I am no longer anticipating the next military invasion. My family and I no longer struggle to put food on the table to simply survive from one season to the next. Light-skinned, educated and North American, I am now among the privileged of the Earth. The time has come, the wren tells me, to de-colonize my mind and to rage when I need to, weep when I must and sing loud and clear when I am called to do so. Why has this last one been the hardest of all for me? From the winter wren of these mossy slopes, I can learn to express the feelings that well up inside of me when the sun rises to warm the forest with coral light.

I return to the creek to my meditation. Once again, I sit and close my eyes. I listen to the creek burbling past my feet. I empty my mind of all thoughts. Empty my body of lingering tremors and aches. Empty my pockets of mundane details and irresolvable worries. Let them swirl away with the water. I take a deep breath of the clear air and let the feathery summer warmth sift down from the treetops into my flesh. Emptying my mind of *all* thoughts, I arrive in this place. I listen now for the wren's song. I do not struggle to avoid the "distraction" of its glee nor to hear the "structure" of the melody. I enter into the song, abandon myself to its exuberance, allowing it to fill me, run like liquid joy through my veins.

I return to my day's work peaceful *and* happy. Joy, passed on to me from the bird I love, helps me stand taller, live more fully. Thanks pal. May I do as much for you.

Fish Out of Water

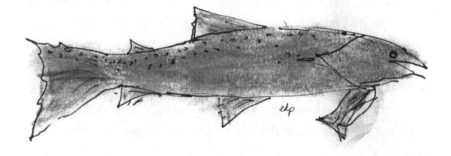

Eileen

It's easy to forget that the Columbia River links the mountain region of its birthplace with the ocean, where it ends. It's also easy to forget that the Columbia Mountains once provided copious spawning grounds for ocean salmon before the construction of Grand Coulee Dam in Washington State. I like to reconstruct in my mind the watershed as it existed long ago, from its source high in the Purcell Range to the outlet of its flow at Astoria, Oregon. In my visual restoration of its pre-dam state, the Columbia River journeys through coastal floodplain and forestland, desert and high mountains. It floods rapidly in spring and summer, then slows and even freezes in autumn and winter. I envision salmon fry carried along the spring flood waters to the sea. I see mature salmon return, swimming up against the river's current toward their birthplace. The spawning salmon surge through the scenic Columbia Gorge and overcome the massive spectacle of Celilo Falls. They swim further and further north, through Priest Rapids and Rock Island Rapids and over Kettle Falls. Along the way, many end their journey where their ancestors dictated. Others swim harder and further, surging up into the steep, blue coolness of the Columbia Mountains, where they encounter the Little Dalles, Steamboat Rapids and the Dalles des Morts. They nestle their eggs in clean gravel, to die for the next generation. Two thousand kilometers from the ocean, the last of the salmon arrive home to Columbia Lake.

Sinixt oral history accounts for the miracle of an ocean salmon finding its way deep into the mountains in what was an unlikely and immensely challenging journey. According to the Sinixt, Coyote released the ocean salmon from a trap that was being watched over by five sisters near the mouth of the river. Coyote led the salmon upstream. When he grew hungry along the way, he called a salmon onto the beach, clubbed it over the head, cooked and ate it. Then he carefully returned the bones to the water, so that the fish could come back to life and swim further into the heartland of the northwest. Of course Coyote had more than one sort of appetite. So, whenever he arrived in a village of people along the Columbia, he offered salmon in trade for a beautiful wife. If a tribe was unwilling to trade, as some-times happened, he placed a barrier in the river, a waterfall too high for the salmon to overcome. In the Columbia Mountains, Bonnington Falls near Nelson kept ocean salmon from ascending to Kootenay Lake. The salmon had free passage everywhere else. Salmon surged by the hundreds of thousands into the narrow valleys of the upper Columbia River and its tributaries.

Today, the presence of salmon in the region has just about passed out of living memory. Few people can recall the fact that salmon spawned here. No one remembers waiting with harpoon or fishing rod for the annual return of chinook in June, sockeye in July and coho in autumn. No one can describe what it was like to watch the fish smell their way to clean spawning grounds on the Columbia, the Kootenay, the Slocan, the Incomappleux and on up to the headwaters. Salmon once acted as a connective tissue of this landscape, linking the ocean to dense mountains, feeding a vast web of life in the process.

Coyote's salmon trade and the annual journey of the fish came to an abrupt end in 1941, when the U.S. Bureau of Reclamation completed the Grand Coulee Dam, barring the salmon from reaching Canadian waters ever again. The dam caused complete extinction of genetic stocks capable of making the long journey, and the Canadian government did nothing to intervene. Several years earlier, when plans for the dam were approved by both the U.S. and Canada, Canadian representatives on the International Joint Commission signed off Canadian interests in the ocean fish. Canada had no commercial fishery to preserve in the Columbia Mountains. Though the fish had provided sustenance for the Sinixt and their neighbours for millennia, they were considered inferior for eating by many settlers. Canadian interest in a commercial salmon fishery focused on the coast, where fish could be caught at the start of their spawning run, rather than further along their journey. The salmon in these mountains were not worth saving.

In addition, with a world at war, power produced by generators at the Grand Coulee Dam began fueling the kilowatt-hungry manufacture of aluminum, in factories building planes to use in the fight for democracy. The United States and Canada were emerging from a Great Depression. Inexpensive electricity and water for drought-stricken farm communities seemed the only way out of a very difficult time. These interests quickly overwhelmed the interests of a fish in coming home. The salmon had no voice, no power and no apparent place in the bright future of the upper Columbia Basin.

From the first day I heard about the historic presence of salmon, I have felt tugged back into the past to understand what the region felt like and looked like when the fish were able to come home. I have wanted to understand the long and arduous journey of the salmon, though I am not sure what has fueled my obsession with this story, unless it is something personal as well. Since my mother fell ill with Alzheimer's Disease and my father died in the late 1990s, I return to my childhood home in California several times a year. This trip involves a drive south to Spokane, then a plane flight. At times, it feels like an odyssey that connects the arid savannah with the interior rainforest, the U.S. with Canada, my childhood with my adulthood, one self with another.

One day in June, as I return to Canada after another weekend away, I find myself contrasting my own personal odyssey across landscapes with the journey of the salmon, fish finding their way unassisted against the current through a vast watershed. As I drive, I entertain myself with the vision I have reconstructed of the salmon swimming home. The size and scope of their journey humbles me and puts into perspective the fatigue I feel as I return to my chosen home. I pass through Spokane traffic and plunge into the fertile Colville Valley. What do I have to be tired about? Imagine the fish and their tireless journey of 2,000 kilometres, over waterfalls, through rapids, into mountains. I have, almost without thinking, chosen a slightly longer route home, one that will take me not directly north, but north and then west, so that I can follow the Columbia drainage into Canada. At the Colville valley's western edge, I catch up with the Columbia River at Kettle Falls, a place the Sinixt called Big Falls, one of the largest salmon fisheries for First Nations in the Pacific Northwest.

I park the car and walk through the woods to the edge of the reservoir formed by the Grand Coulee Dam, Lake Roosevelt. Here, Big Falls once filled the air with mist and noise. Tribes from several nations — the Spokane, the Skoyelpi, the Kalispel, the Sinixt and many others once gathered at these falls to position their J-shaped basket traps. Salmon attempting to leap the falls often fell back into the traps. During the height of the run, the baskets gathered hundreds of salmon a day. No hungry person was turned away in a place where two rules governed: respect for the fish and generosity. Everyone, regardless of tribal affiliation, shared the riches of the river. The fishery was carefully managed to insure future returns, with elaborate rules about conduct around the river and much prayer and meditation on the part of the Salmon Chief before he signaled the start of the harvest.

In the summer of the last salmon runs over Big Falls and home to the Columbia Mountains, Interior Salish tribes from the Colville Reservation gathered near Colville to hold the Ceremony of Tears, a farewell to the age-old cultural practice of salmon fishing on the Columbia that they knew would not be possible the following year. The Sinixt set up one last time on Hayes Island upstream of the falls. This island, always their traditional resting place during the fishing season, is now under water. Photos from the Ceremony of Tears show somber faces of the native people. An audiotape at the Spokane Museum of Arts and Culture plays the reaction of elders as they contemplate what many said could never happen: the end of salmon runs. Their voices crack with emotion. Long pauses interrupt their words. Grief congregates in the back eddy of their speech. The faces and words of these few people hint at the enormous cultural loss experienced by all of the tribes that fished the river for its plentiful ocean food.

Today, the falls, too, are completely submerged. I walk through a grove of mature ponderosa pines along the bluff above the old site of the falls, crushing under my sandals the long, rusty needles that have formed a dense carpet. I follow the forest to the edge of the bluff where I look across the reservoir to the north. Here, in an open area, the Hudson's Bay Company constructed Fort Colville as a trade centre for furs, in 1825. They chose to place the fort very near to the aboriginal fishery, to capitalize on the natural gathering place for many tribes. Archibald McDonald took over as head of the fort in the early 1840s. He had little understanding of the intricate cultural practices surrounding the aboriginal fishery, practices developed over millennia to maintain a consistent supply of the salmon. Letters he left behind make that clear. "There is no want of salmon now at the falls," he wrote to missionaries at another fort on the 15th of June, 1841, "& had the lazy hounds offered such a blessing been only half so industrious as they ought, they might have lain up a good standby before the time they say their creed will allow them to commune."

The Salmon Chief led the fishery with an understanding that successful future years depended on knowing when the time to begin the harvest was right. He conducted the ceremony of the first fish with great reverence, returning to the water the bones of the first salmon caught, just as Coyote had taught. He waited until many fish had moved north above the falls, insuring that they would be able to return home. Macdonald's words indicate ignorance of the ceremony and the reverent conduct that governed the use of the fishery at Big Falls. On the 7th of July, Macdonald wrote again to the missionaries, saying that "the main river began to fall about 25th [of June] and the

Indians have thought it a wise plan to stop further [delaying] in the business of the salmon; the Basket is made and the fish jump in to their heart's content." Macdonald appears to misunderstand the difference between acceptance of natural patterns and laziness, between ecological management and taking whatever is available, whenever one wishes.

I turn away from Kettle Falls and drive farther north, following the shores of Lake Roosevelt. As I move toward the International Boundary, the effect of the dam 250 kilometres downstream becomes less apparent. The reservoir begins to act more like a river, with a sweep of current and varied flow that seem almost hospitable to a fish in search of home. As I drive, I wonder if it is possible to connect two disparate parts of my self, as the salmon connect the ocean with the mountains.

I follow the Columbia's main channel upstream on the road that parallels its passage and bring the picture of the entire watershed back into my mind. The only divisions in the image are natural ones: waterways, mountain ranges, canyons and steep falls. There are no political borders. I want to feel in the depths of the water for the salmon's most natural history, to understand their desire to come home. I have been told that salmon don't have feelings, that they cannot experience desire. But something about their journey signals to me a passionate urge, a compulsion beyond mere instinct. I try to conceive the colour of the water they swam in, the scent of the stones they passed. They must have been tired as they approached what we now call Canada, those that successfully avoided the basket traps at Big Falls.

I slow down to cross the border at Waneta, B.C., where a small, official building perches on a bluff overlooking the Columbia. Here, just beyond Northport, Washington, Lake Roosevelt comes to an end and the Columbia becomes a river again. Opposite the customs counter, large windows look out to freely flowing water. The rippling current catches the June sun.

"Can I take a canoe across the border on the river?" I ask the Canada Customs agent.

The agent regards me with a mixture of suspicion and disdain.

"Yes," he says cautiously. I can tell he wonders why I would be asking.

"Do you enforce the border by boat?" I ask.

"You bet," he replies.

This concern on the part of the Canadian government about what passes back and forth on the river did not, in the 1930s, apply to fish. Just before the Grand Coulee Dam was completed, U.S. survey numbers estimated that 360,000 chinook alone were running up the mid-Columbia to spawn. Many of these would have come north across what is today the 49th parallel to reach the higher tributary streams in Canada. The chinook is known more commonly in the U.S. as spring or king salmon, aptly named for its commanding size of 22 kilograms or more. Chinook prefer to spawn in larger, mainstem rivers. Rivers like the Upper Columbia, which lost nearly half a million fish in 1941.

After my exchange with the border guard, I realize that, unlike a chinook salmon, I will be watched if I try to navigate the water crossing the border. I don't really care to explore the river under the gaze of a uniformed officer, and today anyway, I am without a boat. I drive slowly over the metal bridge spanning the Pend d'Oreille River, a tributary that feeds the Columbia and also once hosted salmon. Now the Pend d'Oreille passes with noisy fury through the concrete gates of the Waneta Dam. I park the car in a wide spot on the road just beyond the bridge and climb out to survey the waters of the Columbia passing below.

The stretch of Columbia River water between this confluence and the Keenleyside Dam nearly 20 kilometres upriver is one of two remaining free-running portions of a waterway 2,000 kilometres long. This small slice of river forms less than one percent of the Columbia's entire journey. In the sunlight, the river glistens with energy and movement. I can almost see here how its power would have daunted early explorers, then later inspired the great hydro systems which now stall its flow over a dozen times on the way to the sea. As I stand before this free fragment, I feel for ghosts of the salmon. Streaked with rainbow colours by the effort of the spawn, the fish would have once teemed unimpeded across this border, continuing up the Columbia to probe high into the mountains as far north as Revelstoke, then farther still, around the Big Bend and all the way to what some say is the source of the river, Columbia Lake.

In 1807, David Thompson and his party of explorers camped near Columbia Lake, feasting on salmon for three weeks. In the 1880s, trophy hunter and explorer Baille-Grohman described the stench of rotting salmon in this area as discernible from kilometres away. A few hundred river kilometres south and almost 200 years after Thompson arrived, I see only a handful of ponderosa pines gathered quietly on the hillsides. The river sends a clean breeze up the cliff. Faintly, over the whine of cars passing on the highway, I hear the river's voice. *The salmon are gone,* it says in watery passing. *The salmon are gone.*

On the road again, I twist along the asphalt toward home, passing Trail, B.C., where the vegetation on the dramatic mountains rising around the town has only recently recovered from sulfur dioxide emissions produced by the Cominco smelter. The river still holds the weight of mining waste. It has had great trouble washing itself clean of the 400 tonnes of slag washed into the Columbia daily for 90 years before clean-up began in 1994. The effects of this pollution are only beginning to be measured and may never be fully understood.

Environmental impacts on salmon stocks, sadly enough, will not be relevant in the discussion, though surely the slag once affected the passage of the fish.

A few kilometres farther east, I arrive at the Columbia's confluence with the Kootenay River, an ancient place called *kp'ítl'els*. Some of the salmon, in particular the sockeye, would have moved east from here up the Kootenay toward the Slocan River drainage, headed for Slocan Lake. Many others, mostly chinook, turned north toward the Lower Arrow Lake, destined for spawning grounds in the Arrow Lakes Valley, north of Revelstoke and beyond the Big Bend. At the confluence, the Sinixt hosted the Secwepemc and the Ktunaxa among others — for fishing and trading. Alex Christian, the last known member of a Sinixt family to live at this spot, described his family as living here for a very long time. Archeological digs report remains carbon-dated to 5,000 plus years.

Several kilometres up the Columbia's main from the confluence looms Hugh Keenleyside Dam (1968), built almost 30 years after the salmon ceased to return. This dam's legacy is not the extirpation of fish, but instead the tragic flooding of historic and prehistoric communities, among them nearly 150 archeological sites of the Sinixt and 32,000 acres of rich valley bottomland. Authorized by the Columbia River Treaty signed between the U.S. and Canada, the Hugh Keenleyside Dam did not have the capacity to produce power until just after the new millennium. Originally, the dam's purpose was to store water, 8.8 billion cubic metres of water to facilitate and maximize U.S. power production at the Grand Coulee and other dams on the system.

I follow the highway east past Castlegar, linking up with the Kootenay River, where the Brilliant Dam (1944) blocks the water in a narrow canyon. East of the Brilliant Dam, more dams stair-step the Kootenay River: the Corra Linn, the South Slocan, the Upper and then

Lower Bonnington, all built within less than 50 kilometres of each other. West Kootenay Power and Light, a subsidiary of Cominco, constructed all of these dams between the end of the nineteenth century and the middle of the twentieth, in order to produce affordable power for the smelter in Trail, B.C. The Kootenay River's bountiful fish stocks and these dams were like oil and water. Their construction interrupted natural river flow, resulting in the fragmentation and isolation of populations that once depended on fast-moving water and specific, seasonal levels for spawning. Bull trout, kokanee, burbot and sturgeon now struggle to survive. For all the fish, dams are the most effective borders of all.

Weeks later, I scramble along the banks of the Kootenay River at Bonnington Falls. I am in search of Coyote's mark, the natural stone pillar imbedded with the spirit of the trickster who first placed the barrier across the river. Today, a concrete arch for Lower Bonnington Dam dwarfs the 10 metre shelf of rock that once formed the falls. I stand at the base of Coyote's rock for a while, asking myself what he must think of the tricks industrial development has played on the landscape. Then, I trace my way a few kilometres downriver, to walk my dogs in the woods near the mouth of the Slocan River, just below the South Slocan Dam and the Kootenay Canal Generating Station. I make this short journey by land, not water. The closely placed dams make water travel hazardous, if not impossible. Danger signs and warnings about sudden surges in water level mark the streamside. Barbed wire fencing prohibits public access to beaches.

The salmon ascending the Kootenay River knew about Coyote's barrier. Before they reached Bonnington Falls, they found other paths to home. Some swirled in Slocan Pool and spawned there. Others turned north up the Slocan River, toward Slocan Lake. Near Slocan Pool, I find my way down to the water's edge. This was once a foam of white water and back-eddy current. Today it spreads into a peaceful wash, wrapping around the small hump of land called Whitely's Island (or Indian Island). Gold Island, an even smaller island where the Sinixt once buried their dead, sits under water now, flooded by the Brilliant Dam. On the shore, a cedar-hemlock forest grows as it once might have. Shadowed paths weave through bits of false box and Oregon grape and a few decaying fir trunks sink slowly into the soil. In places, the ground feels like a damp sponge beneath my shoes, suggesting regular decay, undisturbed over decades. The dogs bound ahead of me as I step around the recessed areas that mark the site of semi-subterranean dwellings of a Sinixt village.

The Sinixt call this area *snt'ekwlítkw*, "much river food." Much River Food was once a heavily populated settlement in the vicinity of Slocan Pool and the mouth of the Slocan River. I follow the dogs through the mature trees of Much River Food before heading down to the water, where I stand quietly for a while. Within moments, I hear a trout flick its tail against the smooth water. Just beyond the bay, this silent water absorbs the still vital, undammed Slocan River. Once the noisy Slocan greets the dammed Kootenay, it, too, will cease to speak.

The word Slocan derives from *slhu7kin*. This Sinixt word for the entire region surrounding the Slocan River translates as "pierce, strike on the head,'" the term for harpooning salmon. Strike on the Head. Much River Food. Anyone who traces archeological sites around the region can see a pattern emerge. Major villages were always on the path of the salmon. Salmon supplemented wild meats, were easily harvested, and could be preserved for winter survival.

In 1826, William Kittison of the Hudson's Bay Company travelled past the mouth of the Slocan River and noted the presence of what he called a "barrier" in the river, a weir constructed to stop the salmon so that they could be easily harpooned. Where there were no deep waterfalls but still lots of fish, as at the mouth of the Slocan River and at the confluence of the Kootenay and Columbia, the Sinixt often constructed weirs. They called them *ntpitkwtn*, "blocking the water." These weirs were made of tripod poles driven into the river bottom at equal distances, with cross poles balanced in the crotches. Once the tripods and cross pieces were in place, a lattice of red-osier dogwood saplings and rope made from hemp dogbane completed the barrier. To construct a weir like this required the cooperation of all members of the village.

The dogs rustle behind me, their tags tinkling in the quiet air. Another trout jumps in the still water. The sun stains it with light. I can only imagine the voices of Sinixt children holding the saplings in place while women secure them with fibrous rope. The voices of men heaving a Douglas fir pole into position across the span of the river The sound of the current fighting the progress of the fish, or the meaty thwack of a harpoon entering the flesh. *Slhu7kín*. A harpoon, piercing food. *Slocan*. I imagine the smell of smoke rising from beneath the racks where salmon were laid to dry.

In 1910, a settler named Robert Elliot landed a chinook salmon very close to the spot where I stand. It fought for an hour and a half, weighed 22 kilograms and measured one and a third metres. A chinook who belonged to this place, a fish who came home. I listen for Elliot's cry of elation, but hear only the hum of the power generators at the South Slocan Dam just upstream.

One day near the end of September, I paddle across the West Arm of Kootenay Lake to a creek where kokanee spawn. Every year, I take a canoe across the Arm to this spot, to remind myself how wild streams below Bonnington Falls might have looked long ago as they surged with salmon from the sea. I slide my canoe up against the sandy shore and step out. At my feet is a dead kokanee. The word kokanee derives from the Sinixt dialect word for the fish, *kukeni*. The Sinixt called them "redfish" and gathered them from creeks each autumn. I know from this dead fish that I will find spawners upstream, flashing their red skirts in the current.

I remove my shoes and walk, carefully, through the deep water near the outflow. I climb out as soon as I can so as not to disturb the spawning beds and hop across boulders before settling onto a stretch of dry gravel. Above me, a raven squawks in a cottonwood. Beside me, in the topaz water, dozens of the redfish point upstream. They are, scientifically, the same species as the ocean sockeye (*Oncorhynchus kisutch*). A portion of ocean sockeye began after the most recent glaciation to confine their life cycles to the fresh waters of the Interior, staying in a lake for their entire adult lives rather than the two years of the ocean species. These are the kokanee, a living reflection of a distant ocean connection. They are the only salmon the Columbia Mountains still have.

All sockeye — whether they live in entirely freshwater like the kokanee or journey for a few years of their lives to the ocean and back — flush bright red as they approach their home streams. Science says that hormonal action triggers the shift of colour, drawing the pigment up from the interior flesh to the exterior skin. I wonder if the change in colour has something to do with coming home. I can't help but think that the sockeye's return has drawn its beauty and passion to the surface. Again it feels to me as if the feelings of the fish are involved. I tell myself sternly, again, that fish do not have feelings or anything that might be mistaken for passion. But I doubt my own words, as I watch the kokanee fight the current, flicking their tail fins in the gravel to prepare spawning beds and deposit eggs. I associate their annual autumn spawn with warm noon times and cold nights, swirling leaves and the ripeness of wild fruit, shadows growing longer, an urgency in the light and in the Earth's many movements.

In the weeks following my paddle across the lake to the kokanee creek, the deciduous trees on the mountain opposite my home flame with gold, illuminating the familiar evergreen slopes with a tapestry of larch, alder and birch. The apples on our backyard tree hang heavy in the tangle of branches, blushing with sweetness as the woodpile beneath them grows. One night, bundled in sweaters on our patio at dusk, my husband and I see a dark form slide across our lawn, a black bear headed for the compost bin. The dogs sitting upwind of the bear do not stir. Now is the time that bears search for food, when they fatten as much as they can. It is the time when they enter the town, especially the young adults, to gain what they can to survive another winter. This bear does not stay long, before heading quickly up the bank behind us and on toward the mountain forests only a few blocks uphill.

Not long after, I dream of an emaciated bear driven out of hibernation by its own hunger. The fur of the animal hangs loosely on its large, broad-shouldered frame. Portions of its digestive organs trail on the ground behind it. It looks desperate, weak and confused. The dream troubles me for days. I walk in the autumn woods, thinking about bears preparing for winter, bears unseen within the trees. The wind circles through the cedar and hemlock forest surrounding a

181

creek near my home. A few birch leaves dance across the air. Elder-berry shrubs offer umbrellas of frosted, blue fruit. I step across bear scat laced with the red-orange hulls of mountain ash berries. I find a young mountain ash tree, one of its lower branches snagged roughly at the base. Torn leaves and bits of berry stem litter the ground.

Before the construction of Grand Coulee Dam, bears would have found their way to the shores of the water one last time in October, to pluck up the coho with clumsy paws. They would have known that the coho were the last salmon to run up from the ocean before winter began. In the course of their adult life, anadromous salmon destined to come home to the mountains gathered copious amounts of marine protein before they entered the river's path. The fish bore a molecular signature: the nitrogen molecule 15N, a heavy nitrogen isotope found most abundantly in oceans. This nitrogen is a potent food. In coastal regions where salmon runs still exist, up to 75 percent of the total nitrogen found in vegetation up to 150 metres on either side of spawning streams can be traced to 15N. The ocean feeds the land via the fish, which transfers its life from salt to fresh water, then to soil.

Recently, the bones of a very old grizzly bear were excavated in the mountains here and analyzed for nitrogen content. Ninety percent of the bear's nitrogen was of marine origin, the heavy 15N carried to the region by the salmon. The effects of salmon extinction in the region would have been felt strongly by the bears. In 1941, when they came looking for the salmon starting in June, they would not have found any. I imagine paws swiping the river water and coming up empty. Again and again, empty. To survive, bears would have eaten more berries, or dug desperately for more grubs, or searched for a kokanee stream. They might have raided a grain bin in a barn, angering a farmer preparing for winter himself. They certainly would have gone to sleep hungry, woken even hungrier and perhaps not lived to see another season.

The kokanee, now fed artificially by fertilizer tanks that float on the lakes of the region to compensate for nutrients trapped behind dams, are beginning to repopulate freshwater aquatic systems in the Columbia Mountains. At the creek I like to visit, I have seen steady increases in the number of fish returning over the past several years. Since volunteers altered a culvert for a rail line that crosses the creek, even more have penetrated higher up the creek. This is good news, but it still only amounts to a few hundred fish. At Kokanee Creek Provincial Park, the creek bed is carefully managed for optimum gravel size and water flow. Thousands of kokanee return every year to spawn. Yet even these successful numbers shrink in magnitude compared to the hundreds of thousands of anadromous salmon who once came home.

While political and environmental leaders discuss more and more realistically the possible dismantling of one or more dams along the Snake River system in the U.S. to restore salmon stocks, no one has yet proposed the dismantling of the Grand Coulee Dam, or the construction of a fish ladder to facilitate passage of the chinook, sockeye or coho back to their Canadian home. Given the extinction of the genetic stocks that once swam this far, the likelihood of salmon being restored to these mountains seems all but scientifically impossible. Such a decision would require an enormous shift in values by our culture, or the discovery of a more plentiful, more economical source of energy than hydro-power.

Many native people view the dams as entirely temporary. A common story among First People of the Interior Plateau tells of Coyote eventually departing the region. Before he left, the story goes, he made a promise to the people of the land: no matter what, he would live on. *I will be back*, he said to the people. Interior Salish elders prophesy that when Coyote does return, he will remove all the industrial dams from the path of the salmon, much as he once dismantled the traps the five sisters built at the mouth of the Columbia. Coyote gave the fish passage across the land. He once helped them find a home. Perhaps he can do so again.

Come back, Coyote. Come back.

Illuminating the Unseen

K. Linda

 A week ago, my land partner Joe looked out her living room window and saw a cougar sauntering up our driveway. "Sauntering," she repeated when I talked to her on the phone. "Its legs were so long. It was huge — it walked like it owned the place."

 The cat was headed toward my house. For so many years, I have wanted to see a cougar. Here one was, on its way past my door; unfortunately, I was away and thus missed my opportunity to watch the great dun-coloured lion meander by. After 25 years in the Columbia Mountains, Joe's cougar-sighting number had finally come up. We had seen the tracks of a cougar and kitten once before on our land, but this was the first sighting in the flesh.

Hoping to see a cougar is like revelling in a violent thunderstorm. There's a right time and place for such things and if it does happen, it can be either a rapturous moment or a frightening abyss. Like with a storm, one hopes to encounter a cougar in the safety of shelter. One hopes that one's domestic animals are indoors and that the cougar moves on, not remaining in the area to hunt. A cougar sighting, especially close to home, remains with people, even with those who didn't witness the cat's passage itself. The knowledge that a large predator, one up the food chain from humans, is in our midst lingers like a powerful odour that brings a heightened alertness to all our senses. It reminds us of our vulnerability.

I return home a few days after the cougar sighting. As I climb out of the truck, I peer carefully into the woods around my house, both cautious and curious. What if a cougar's steady gaze were to meet mine from among the abundant May foliage? Of course, there is no cougar conveniently waiting to greet me. There is no way of even knowing if the cougar is still in our neck of the woods. It could be tracking our movements as we go from house to garden to road. Or it could be hundreds of kilometers away. Nevertheless, over the days that follow, I walk through the woods full of the realization that I am potential prey. I feel both humbled and strangely exhilarated. The presence of a predator nearby reminds me in the deepest way possible that I do not control my fate. It reminds me that there are many parts to being wild. As I try to go about my daily activities in my usual way, I catch myself thinking: Can I make room for all of what wildness entails in my notion of home?

Our worst instinctual fear as animals is to be eaten. Even though we are much more likely to be killed in a car accident or die of an environmentally-induced disease, the human animal has not evolved to fear these things. Yet the low incidence of cougar attacks on humans does not substantiate our fear. In the 100-year period from 1890 to 1990, there were only 53 cougar attacks on humans. Only 10 of these resulted in death to humans. Even though more than half of these attacks happened in British Columbia — Vancouver Island being a hotspot — these numbers are still tiny compared with other causes of human death, even in the animal realm. Each year in North America, tens of people are killed by dogs and bees, and over a hundred humans perish in deer-related car accidents. However, in each of these cases, humans are simply killed, not eaten and thus, fear of the predator still holds the upper hand.

Many human civilizations have made it their work to eliminate predators, perhaps in hopes of eliminating this fear. By 1900, cougars had been extirpated from Eastern North America. During the first half of the twentieth century, at least 20,000 cats were killed in B.C., leaving many areas denuded of their top predator. But as populations of predators dwindle, we also seem to miss the heightened state of consciousness that being hunted brings. Some people seek out the growing body of books on grizzly, cougar and other predator attacks on humans. Others flirt with increasingly dangerous adrenaline sports. Still others fill the cinemas, quivering in their seats as Hollywood's latest horror fantasy plays itself out in Technicolor.

I am not prone to seeking out fear. Though no one would call me a wuss, I avoid violence and experience a weakening of my legs when confronted with juicy flesh wounds. Why is this? Is it how I have positioned myself on the food chain? In addition to the fact that my species sits below the great meat-eating mammals in the hierarchy, I myself am a vegetarian of 25 years, a joiner of collectives and cooperatives, an anarchist with no liking for hierarchies and from a pacifist-minded people. I have never cultivated an affinity for the hunt, for stalking and the chase, for pouncing and digging my teeth into flesh.

I have always, consciously or subconsciously, turned away from anything to do with bloody, torn carcasses and the large, pointed canine teeth that do this work. That is, until this cougar walked past my house in broad daylight.

Now, the thought of the cougar walks through my days with me. As I enter into the knowledge of its presence, curiosity carries me away from fear, toward something else. My heightened awareness of my surroundings reminds me of how animals who are prey species — including humans — have evolved in response to predation. Our large brains, for example, have developed not just to increase our ability to acquire food and shelter, but also to avoid becoming food. Will we, as a species, retain our competitive edge if we no longer have predators to hone our minds against? Will we, as humans, survive the unbalancing of our food chain, or will we soil our collective nest and eat ourselves out of house and home like a warren of rabbits with no owls or coyote to keep them in check?

Could it be that, as humans, we need predators to maintain the ecosystems in which we live as much as any other species? Ecologists have discovered that each species of plant and animal not only withstands the activities of the other species with which it co-exists, but also evolves and thrives based on those activities. The tightly linked relationships that exist in ecosystems are just that: relationships. When predators are removed, an ecosystem veers out of balance from the top down, the effect of its absence spreading over its entire territory, as pervasively as a lack of rain, permeating right down to the roots of the grasses. It is not a role that we can simply replace, through human activities. We can declare that we humans are now at the top of the predator heap, but it doesn't necessarily make it so. The role that predators play in ecosystems goes far beyond the act of eliminating other animals.

When a cougar hunts, for example, it provides for a community far bigger than itself and its own kind. After downing a deer and snapping its spinal cord with a surgically placed bite, a cougar will feed in a methodical way. Because it can only eat up to five kilograms at a time, it starts with the prime organs — heart, liver and lungs. It leaves the rest of the carcass for further feedings over the days to come, dragging it to a sheltered location and covering it with forest debris. Before it returns for its next meal, bears, coyotes, ravens and other mammals and birds will gather and share its kill. Eventually, the mice, voles, beetles and maggots will have their fill as well. Finally, the bones and hide, as well as the excrement of all those who have feasted, will fertilize the forest floor.

It is one thing to know that being predated upon is a vital part of the Earth's functioning. It is another thing to meet it face on, in the shape of a two metre long, 70 kilogram feline, who is exclusively carnivorous, padding nonchalantly past one's house. When I sit down at the creek in the morning to meditate, I scan the slopes of the creek gully before I close my eyes. I open my eyes more often to check out any unusual sounds. It is hard to forget that there are unseen eyes in this forest and that those eyes might be upon me. And though I've been known to say I'd rather be eaten by a cougar than die in a car crash, I don't feel quite ready to make that final journey. After a week of heightened alertness and reading about the cougar, my thoughts shift away from being prey. One morning, as I return from the creek, I catch myself looking at the woods in a new way: as the cougar might.

Cougars are able to see well night and day and their eyes have large visual fields of view of up to 290 degrees. Their eyes are mounted in front, like human eyes, to provide for the most highly developed binocular vision of any carnivore. This helps them judge distances so that they can plan a precise hunting strategy. Their finely tuned hearing picks up the cautious steps of deer or other prey moving through the underbrush. Their heavy musculature and light skeleton are built for speed and agility, and their spectacularly long, snaky tail helps them balance. A cougar can leap 14 metres horizontally and jump five metres into the air. Up in our abandoned apple orchard, I calculate these distances on the ground, then stand, staring in disbelief and awe at what the cougar is capable of. With skills like these, it is no wonder that cougars hunt opportunistically, meaning they take those animals easiest to take. A cougar has nothing to prove, just an empty belly to fill or growing kittens to nourish. It occupies its niche with the natural grace of one who belongs.

When I think of the cougar like this — as one who belongs — I am confronted with the question of the way in which I belong to this place. The Sinixt and other First Peoples of similar ecosystems were all hunting people. Though they knew they weren't the fiercest hunters in the forest, they were well aware of their own predatory nature. For this reason, many First Peoples of the Americas revered the cougar. Stone-carved fetishes of mountain lions were used to aid hunters and lion parts were used in ritual and medicine. Among the expansionist and warlike Inca, rulers hunted cougar to add to their prestige. Unlike the bear who was often referred to as sister or uncle, the cougar has rarely been family or peer to indigenous people in the Americas. With its place on the food chain clearly *above* humans, the cougar has been a dangerous but captivating stranger to watch out for.

The cougar has never been hunted for food or clothing. If it is hunted by people of North American settler cultures, it is hunted out of fear, as a scapegoat, or to appease our hunger for status. Alive, the cougar is competition for modern humans who claim a place at the pinnacle of the food chain. But humans make a strange claim to that

190

place at the top of the hierarchy: we want the top, but we don't want to be seen as predators. We apply the term "predator" to child molesters and men who are so-called womanizers. It is not meant to flatter. We don't even want to think of ourselves as carnivores. As a vegetarian of 25 years, I've borne witness to the defensiveness and discomfort of many a meat eater. In my more confrontational youth, I'd ask fellow non-vegetarian diners how they were enjoying their roast carcass and then watch them squirm. Calling their meat corpse or cadaver did not win me popularity points. Grocery stores have colluded with people in their avoidance of their carnivorous tendencies through the sanitized cellophane and Styrofoam of meat counters. We do not want to look at the once live animal that died so that we can eat. We want to paint ourselves as more benign creatures than we have proven ourselves to be. But what would happen if we owned our own predatory nature?

As I roam my home woods, hunting for signs of the visiting cougar — scratches on trees, scat, strange odours, remains of kills — I discover there's more of a predator to me than I had originally thought. My reading on predators and the cougar in particular has led me to a new-found passion for their power, a respect for how a natural hierarchy functions and an understanding of their plight in the human-dominated world. And though the big cat itself leaves me no signs, I begin to feel its presence inside of me. My co-author gives me a startling picture of the face of a cougar. I post it on the bulletin board by my desk and practise looking back into its intense and unwavering blue gaze.

I also borrow a friend's slingshot and practise shooting small stones at a tree. Having never hunted, I begin to wonder how I would choose my prey, which rabbit or grouse would I would be willing to remove from the forest for my supper. The trade-off — one supper for me, a loss of an entire life for the animal — seems harsh, and yet animals like the cougar, wolf, marten, lynx, owl, osprey, and even the shrew and dragonfly, make precisely that trade-off every day. How predators choose their prey is a much studied, much debated question. Whether the hunter selects out the weakest of its prey for the mutual benefit of both species, just takes what it can, or merely responds to a voluntary sacrificial offering made to it by the community of the prey, we will probably never know. We do know that eating and being eaten is what turns the wheel of life for every living being. So why our shame and avoidance?

Is it because we know, on some deep level, that we are not in balance with our environment? That taking life, even if it happens again and again, on a daily basis is an act that requires respect. And that respect is only possible for the humble? Are we afraid that being humble means that we have to face being prey? What would happen if we acknowledged our place on that wheel? Could it be a homecoming back to the wild?

It seems that it has been much easier for us humans, when push comes to shove and we are asked to face our destructive behaviour, to transfer our responsibility to something else, someone else, preferably something or someone that frightens us. In the Columbia Mountains, it is the cougar that has been scapegoated. The great hunter is now the hunted. Not having evolved as prey, its small lungs are inadequate for the endurance required of it these days. In the southern Columbia Mountains in Idaho, there are no limits placed on cougar hunting at all, and hunters are free to use snowmobiles to pursue their quarry. With the increase of roads in most areas, there aren't many places cats can hide anymore. In Idaho and B.C., dogs can be used to hunt cougar. In Washington, they cannot. In all three places, many cats are killed annually through legal hunting or the removal of "problem" animals. The South Selkirk Cougar study lost three of their 16 collared subjects to permitted hunters in a three-year period.

What drives a government's choices about cougar hunting? In the South Selkirk Mountains of B.C., it is, at least in part, politics. Human inhabitation, recreation and industry are devastating what's left of caribou habitat yet it is the cougar the government blames for the rapid dwindling of the caribou herds. Radio-collared cougars in the South Selkirk Mountains were found to rarely prey on caribou. Their main food has and continues to be white-tailed deer and the occasional mule deer or elk. However, clear cutting at higher elevations has been drawing deer populations up higher than they have traditionally grazed and cougars have followed them, bringing the cats into contact with the caribou. One cougar who developed a taste for caribou was subsequently shot by biologists for this transgression. Where in this is there acknowledgement that cougars have existed in balance with caribou populations for centuries if not millennia, whereas the recent boom in back-country ski lodges, extensive snowmobiling, mining, transmission lines, pipelines and logging which fragment caribou habitat has sent the once great caribou herds into an unprecedented decline. Like spotted owls, caribou are a thorn in the side of those who value resource extraction profits over ecological integrity. But this is not a new story, rather one that North American society seems hell-bent on repeating, even here in "Supernatural BC".

It's been a few weeks since the cougar sauntered past Joe's window and up the driveway toward my place. As I mulch the garlic in the garden, I realize I haven't thought of the cat yet today. It's as if my modern psyche can no longer sustain the intensity that being prey requires. I look up into the forest above the garden and try to conjure up the beast. Somehow, the land feels benign, but this is not an entirely good feeling; there is a flatness to it, an emptiness that I had not perceived before. How is it that one predator sighting can carry so much weight when these animals are among us, here in the Columbia Mountains, all the time? That one animal was like a beam of light, shining into an almost forgotten recess of my own wild animal self.

I have no idea where the cougar Joe saw is now, but these great felines are, nevertheless, walking this land, hunting and eating, staking territory and breeding as I go about my day. As invisible to us as air, they are moving among us, not as threats to our safety, but as essential to our lives as breath. Even if we kill every single cougar, we still will not be safe. The most frightening predator is the one we hold within but will not acknowledge. Much as this ecosystem cannot thrive without predators like the cougar, we cannot grow and change until we look our own predatory nature square in the face. And we will not be humbled until, simultaneously, we understand that we are also prey.

Awakening

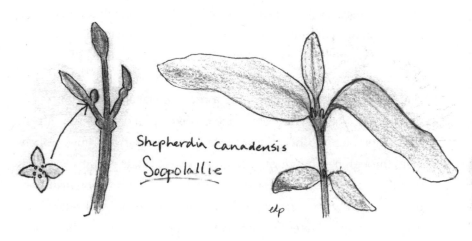

Shepherdia canadensis
Soopolallie

elp

Eileen

In the late winter of 1998, I bought a hard-covered black note-book, a few ink pens and a set of coloured pencils. I wanted to keep an artistic and also somewhat scientific record of the plants growing in the place where I live.

My father gave me a book for my 37th birthday that served as my inspiration: *A Trail through the Leaves, the journal as a path to place.* Hannah Hinchman delights readers with page after page of drawings, paintings, written musings and maps of her home, the Rocky Mountains of Montana. I was and still am entranced by her close attention to her surroundings, by her willingness to express that attention artistically, and, more than anything else, by her ability to allow the natural world to influence her deeply as a human being.

Hinchman's book reflects a more recent cultural movement well established in the U.S., that of cultivating a conscious knowledge of homeplace through the keeping of a naturalist's notebook or journal. The naturalist's notebook has deep roots in the nineteenth century practice of botanical drawings by both amateur naturalists and scientists, and even deeper, in the notebooks of Carl Linneaus, the 18th century "father" of a system of scientific classification for plants still in use today. While knowledge of plants can be a professional activity, a journal of place can also be a joyful record, one carried out in order to develop an appreciation for or connection with one's natural surroundings. Hinchman, through her drawings, maps, notes and colour palettes, explores visually what ecologists today call *bio-regionalism*. Bio-regionalism sees the North American landscape not as a uniform entity, but rather, as a collage of many different regions rubbing up against each other. These regions have their own climates and plants, animals and geography. Bio-regions often defy political boundaries such as state lines, provincial borders, counties, cities and countries, but often parallel or approximate the traditional territories of indigenous people.

Modern styles of North American inhabitation have driven culture and nature farther and farther apart with agricultural settlement, the development of an industrial society that focuses on resource extraction and the spread of the automobile. These practices, among others, have contributed to this separation, distancing those who live in places from interdependence with the biological rhythms of wild plants and animals. When I purchased my hardbound black notebook three years after I arrived in the Columbia Mountains, I knew the names of only a few of the local indigenous plants, other than a few I recognized from the B.C. coast. I could not describe their habitats or their blooming times. I admitted to myself as I thumbed Hinchman's volume that I knew little if anything about the natural place where I lived.

I suppose that *A Trail Through the Leaves* arrived in my life at a time when I most needed to locate myself. I found myself wanting to map the terrain of tight valleys with its angled shadows, the braided network of streams, the placement of various types of rock. And, in the tradition of a field naturalist, I also wanted to sketch systematically the plants that I noticed, recording their Latin (scientific) and common names. Plants, perhaps more than any other element of a natural system, are the most approachable and noticeable expression of a bio-region. I wanted to learn to differentiate a native plant from an introduced one. I wanted to be able to identify trees by looking only at their bark. (I'm still working on that one.) I wanted to learn which plants for the indigenous people were medicinal, which were for food, and which formed part of their hunting and gathering technology. (I'm still working on that one, too.) I wanted to come to know the place where I live, despite the fact that I hadn't held a drawing pen for over a decade. I would just do it. And in the process, I hoped I would learn. I opened the first page of my notebook and dated it: February 16, 1998.

When I began to keep a naturalist's record of place I didn't know how much my close attention to plant life would teach me about my self, about the rhythms of growth and change, about how a landscape *expresses* its own rhythmic pulse on a minute level and in so doing, reflects the human capacity for cyclical breath, repeated thoughts, changeable moods. I found myself identifying more and more with the flowers, trees and shrubs around me. *To bloom is work*, I wrote in bold, block letters early in my notebook, beside a sketch of a nootka rose.

As often as I could, I took myself outdoors: to meet plants, to smell the air, to watch the season shift. I didn't venture far to do this work. Anyplace where wild things grew, I would walk. I would trudge up the steep hill near our house in town to the abandoned railway tracks.

I walked for long distances under the arching shade of evergreens, beneath the white spires of birch, alongside creeks, through the rain. I watched the snow melt back and green shoots emerge. I marvelled at the rain dripping like jewels on the end of branch tips. Whenever I noticed something that interested me, I stopped to sketch it or make a note. The pages from these early walks are often mottled and smeared, either with rainwater, or sometimes, as can happen in a personal exploration, with tears.

Not far away in these same mountains, someone else had begun to study plants with profound curiosity as well. I did not yet know K.Linda Kivi. She did not carry a visual notebook under her arm as I did, but she approached plants with a similar passion, a keen attention to detail and a desire to understand them, as a way of learning to call this place home. Whether one keeps a visual notebook or not, awakening can be witnessed. It can be inspired within us, and experienced through plants growing around us.

K.Linda

I saw it from the car window on my way home from Jake's. On the forest floor, under the tightly laced canopy of hemlocks, the clump of pale growth caught my eye. Though I had never seen this plant before, I knew exactly what it was. The elusive gnome plant! It looked like a cauliflower or a fungus at first glance, its pinkish, waxy stems closely bunched together. The plant rose about 20 centimetres above the bare duff and its scale-like leaves made it look furry. A few buds had opened at the tips of some stems. Their fleshy, four-petalled, creamy cups faced up. The whole plant was totally lacking in green. I put my nose to the blossoms: apples.

Though it is somewhat more common on the coast, the gnome plant pops up in the Columbias in only a few places. The phenomenon, known as "disjunction," is one of the wonders of the Interior Rainforest of the Columbia Mountains. After the last ice age, there was a time when the climate throughout the Pacific Northwest was wet and warm. What we now think of as coastal plants, grew widely around the province. When the weather became drier, the moisture loving plants retreated, mostly to coastal areas. However, some also found refuge here, in our wet valleys, like the oceanic lichens recently found in the Incomappleux valley. They bear witness to the impermanent, shifting nature of ecosystems.

The gnome plant is also the only member of its genus in the world, and botanists aren't always sure which family to place it in. *Monotropaceae? Ericaceae?* It eludes study by surfacing only from time to time. I had been waiting to see the gnome plant since the summer of 1994 when Jake last saw it growing in his forest. This July (2000) was proving warm enough for it to emerge again. What does it do underground all those years?

As a mycotrophic wildflower, it derives all its nutrition from underground instead of photosynthesizing it like most plants. Its emergence is simply a reproductive strategy. (This is likely the source of one of its other common names, the fungus flower.) Perhaps this is why it can afford to wait until conditions are just so before it puts in an appearance. Thriving is not so much about an abundance of numbers or a big presence; it's more about knowing when to put in an appearance and making the best with what you have. I watched the plant for the rest of the summer. It slowly turned brown until it was a rattling clump of hollow stems. I await its return.

Eileen

In March, 1998, on the Spring Equinox during one of my walks, I notice a shrub that looks dead. Its bare branches are reddish brown and its branch tips end in dry, flattened ovals, the shape of praying hands. Around this shrub, the branch tips of other shrubs swell noticeably, but this one seems lifeless. That was perhaps why it first caught my attention. Then, I notice a small flash of electric green at the base of one of the praying hands. I bend closer and see a tiny bloom, a four-pointed, chartreuse star facing the milky sunshine of early spring. *Such a green,* I note beside my sketch, *to have been kept prisoner in tough, brown skin.* I search for more signs of this green on the shrub, but find none.

I return a few days later. More chartreuse stars had begun to twinkle along the branches of the shrub. By now, the plant has my full attention. As I sketch what I see, counting, I realize that the shrub is alive. At home again, I try to identify the plant in a book that had become my constant companion, Parish, Coupe and Lloyd's *Plants of the Southern Interior.* But the small colour photographs in the guidebook, taken in the height of the growing season, cannot help me identify the chartreuse, star-shaped blooms or the speckled brown hands, praying for spring to arrive.

Spring comes to the Columbia Mountains minutely. There is no sudden explosion of blossoms, or instant, reliable warming. Mountains make their own weather, creating cool, changeable winds off snowy ridgelines, rain from moist breezes that rub against steep slopes. March here can be a series of steps forward to warmth, steps back to cold, a dull progression of slushy, dormant days with not much noticeable growth or change in the vegetation. Observed more closely, however, March becomes an awakening of energy, a force rising through dormant plants to burst forth into the world. I didn't see it for years, but with notebook in hand, I began to notice. Pages from that March and early April are filled with sketches of my realization. One page surveys various shapes of leaf buds swelling at the tips of branches. One page sketches as many catkins as I could find, those frothy flowers of willow, hazelnut, alder and birch that emerge long before the leaves. I realize, in the effort to look closer, that even skunk cabbages are in bloom everywhere in the moist bottomlands, their yellow lanterns lighting the soupy muck. They are not a graceful flower, but they bloom at a time when their light is welcomed. I also begin to notice that false solomon's seal was sending up new green spears that if picked, steamed and eaten, taste like asparagus.

The bravery and mystery of early spring evolves into what I decide to call Leafing Out Time. I begin to observe the various shapes of leaves as they open and spread to the warming days. On May 5th, as I walk along the same gravel road, I come across a softly grey-green plant with long, oval leaves and small green fruit clustered near the stems. I had all but forgotten about the strange, chartreuse-coloured stars and the praying hands. But something about the plant draws me to it. As I sketch the leaves, I notice the reddish-brown bark. Where had I seen that before? Then, I lift a leaf and see a pale-brown, speckled underside. A reminder of the praying hands. In the margin, I scribble *Is this the same plant I saw back on March 20?* At home, I cross-reference my basic sketch of the mature leaves with my plant guidebook until I find it: *Shepherdia canadensis*, common name: soopollalli, from the Chinook words for *soap* (soop) *berry (ollali)*. The praying hands, the chartreuse star, the soft green leaves: this is a common, berry-producing shrub. A shrub that likes dry, sunny locations and produces prolific, if bitter red fruit prized by the Sinixt as food.

The scope of spring; the mystery of awakening. A supple shrub emerges from an arrangement of brown sticks peppered with hands clasped in prayer and tiny green stars. Plants are masters of subterfuge. And there is more. More going on in the early spring of our beings than we can possibly record.

K. Linda

Wild ginger, wild, wild, gingery-gee.

Flowers hiding under your evergreen, heart-shaped leaves.
Maroon bloom
three petals spinning from your cupped, creamy centre
a secretive gesture of spring extravagance.
You send out your fragrant, aromatic rhizomes, send them
snaking out into the sweet soil.
I walk across your carpet of green hearts like an empress
treading on
thick Persian rugs,
my tongue aflame with your fire.

Eileen

June. My notebook has worked its way through a fascination with catkin and bud, then leaf, to a fixation on flowers. They open everywhere. I sketch petal shapes, smell the centres, watch the bees drift by unseen clouds of pollen. I pick a tuft of Saskatoon berry flowers and separate one of them from the rest. I sketch it to fill a whole page, then scribble a note across the bottom. *Do any of us look so elegant when viewed alone? How can I remove myself from the cluster?*

Everywhere, flowers burst into bloom. I sketch as many as I can. They are the complex organs of a plant, the most attractive part, the brightest example of quality and beauty. They bloom and I watch them, marveling at the effort it must take to open so widely to the world. Petals spread out bravely, exposing the stamens, the pistils. And then, just as I marvel, the beauty passes. Flowers cannot last forever. Some bloom only for a day and then begin to wilt and fade. Some last longer, but each and every one passes toward fruit eventually.

One cloudy, warm day, I am stopped in my tracks by the beauty of thimbleberry, *Rubus parviflorus*. The Latin name stumbles off my tongue. I transcribe it carefully beside my sketches. *Rubus parviflorus*. Such a jumble of terms, words that do not describe what I see: a plant whose leaves spread wide and lush, a flower in poetic transition between blossom and fruit. The Sinixt term for the thimbleberry fruit is *pálpelk̲n*, or, "always flat-headed." The large, blush-pink petals have begun to wither and at their centre sits the beginning of the broad berry. The individual spikes of pollen have been fertilized into seed, one by one. Beside my sketch, I write *Is a berry many tiny pieces of individual fruit, or is it one whole fruit?* The scientific answer does not seem important, but the philosophical concept of what forms a whole puzzles me for days.

A few weeks later, I find the first huckleberries, pushing quickly from flower to fruit in the suddenly hot weather. *Vaccinium membranaceum*. So many syllables, for a berry the Sinixt call simply *st'xalh̲k* (sweet fruit). These berries on the bush are still very green, but when I bend down to peer even more closely, I see the slightest ring of purple at the base of one globe. *The rim of purple ripeness*, I write in the margin beside the sketch. Sweetness marks its arrival. And with it comes a desire: to seek out the rim of purple ripeness, wherever it can be found.

In early September, 1999, I pluck a stem of wild rose hip from the trail on my way down to a favourite lakeside beach. I can feel in the air that this might be my last swim of the year. The ground in the shaded woods feels cool, even though the sun is still strong. I sit on the warm sand, twirling the stem between my fingers, watching the glistening rose hip catch the long-shadowed light. I wash a blue back-drop on the notebook, trying to separate the sky from the mountain. Then I draw the hip as exactly as I can. Brown, wispy sepals frame the luscious lines of the hip. These sepals were once the flower bud's protective layer. The petals have dropped away, but the old protec-tion of the emerging bloom drapes itself below the husky, lip-red fruit, as a reminder of an earlier phase.

My notebook pages record many conversations between plants and my evolving heart. As I witness the progression between leaf, bloom and fruit, I begin to greet within me the same cycle of open-ing, receiving and ripening. I continue to record diligently the Latin terms as I sketch plant after plant, berry after berry, leaf after leaf. But more and more, I relate to the common names, the indigenous names. They have a sort of expressive power that the Latin names do not have. Often, the common or indigenous names mark more clearly the local bond between culture and nature.

The Latin nomenclature for plants is also known as the Linnaean system. The development of this system was brilliant work that helped systematize plant life into a world order so that anywhere on the globe, a plant could be classified within the same system. A name for the genus, always capitalized, always listed first, signalling a group of common characteristics. Then a name for the species, in lower case, listed second and signalling differences. This process has resulted over time in science squeezing "local knowledge" out of the plant, reducing it to a biological specimen of a whole world system rather than an expression of a precise place.

Yet, the man who authored the system had a direct and personal relationship with plants. According to his mother, Linnaeus preferred as a child to play with flowers rather than toys. He kept intricate, artistic journals of plants even as an adult, and in one entry made when he was a young man, named one plant after the Greek goddess Andromeda, likening "the distressed virgin" goddess and her "blushing face" with the way the "rosy-coloured flower hangs its head." I wonder how Linnaeus would feel about how his system is employed today, with a sort of slavish attention to the objective rather than the subjective, the universal rather than the local.

K. Linda

When locals give names to plants, it is so that they can remember them. Common plant names are intended to evoke images for the people who use the plants and live alongside them. Each plant has a character, a style. I sometimes think of all the Columbia Mountain common plant names that would make great names for bands, because they too want to project a character, a style. Now all I need is a band to name. Perhaps the musicians and I could help each other. Techno, Celtic, pop, classical, world, punk, you name your genre; we'll find a good name in the plant book.

How about: Mock Orange, Twisted Stalk (punk rock), Bear Grass, Lime Dust, Saxifrage (undoubtedly jazz), Prince's Pipe, Sundew (bluegrass), Skunk Cabbage, Bitterroot, Black Sanicle, Death Camas (heavy metal), Wild Sarsparilla, Shepherd's Purse (Celtic), Bastard Toad-Flax, Enchanter's Nightshade (classical), Locoweed (reggae), Devil's Club, Soopolallie, Hound's Tongue (country), Great Burdock, Monkey Flower (hip hop).

Go on you musicians, pick one. Take it. You can have it. There are more.

Eileen

Then there are what I call "plant coincidences," the way a plant just pops up in one's path as if it has a message to offer. The rational mind does not know what to do with these moments.

When I lived on the west coast of B.C., I developed a particular fondness for the plant *Gaultheria shallon*, popularly known as salal. Walking in the forested woods as a young mother of two small boys, I was often surrounded by the shrub's curved branches and leaves draping toward me from all directions. In the dense undergrowth, I began to hear the voices of Coast Salish berry-pickers, the indigenous women who gathered the prolific fruit for winter sustenance and for trade. The curving forms of the berry pickers emerged from the shadows cast by the oval leaves. The prolific spread of the plant spoke of a woman's fecund nature, the call of Mother Earth, the moist *yin*, the *anima*, the soul. Salal represented to me all that any woman could be, if she chose, a berry picker of patience and prolific power, a beautiful presence in the dark and tangled woods.

It never occurred to me when I moved 800 kilometres inland that I would find salal here, in the Columbia Mountains. But like the gnome plant, salal takes advantage of the moistest and most mild corners of this mountain zone, a bioregion that has similarities with the coastal rainforest. When I discovered that salal grew here, too, I wanted to find it. Whenever I walked in drainages that were shaded and cool, wherever the moisture-loving hemlock spread its lacy limbs and grew from soil that sprang in a moist, coastal way beneath my feet, I looked for salal. Once, I was fooled by western tea-berry. It turned out that this related plant was smaller and spread too low to the ground to be the salal I searched for, the call of a woman's presence in the woods.

After a few years of keeping my notebook, I entered a time of full-blown personal crisis. (This was not the fault of the notebook, by the way.) One day in October 2000, on a walk in the woods near Crawford Bay, at the fringe of a small stand of cedar and hemlock forest on a north slope in an open space beside a rock slab, I found a patch of salal the size of a small living room carpet. I crouched down, astonished. The salal was only a foot high, and I could see no sign of berries. Through the tears that had been welling in my eyes, I found something to ease my sadness. The plant reminded me of the possibilities inherent in supple survival and in adaptability. I bent down and ran my hands across the leathery leaves supported by reddish stems. I felt the tough, smooth beauty of the plant, marvelled at its soft curves. My notebook has no entry for that important discovery, other than an undated sketch of the leaf's lovely shape, marked by a smear of green.

I had found salal. Or perhaps, it had found me.

K. Linda

One of my all-time favourite plants is devil's club. I introduce it to everyone who comes to visit me. This is, in part, due to my fondness for it, but more so because of one of its distinctive features: thorns. Devil's club has some of the most fearsome, potent thorns ever invented by nature. Not only are they long, fine and sharp, but once pricked, they exude a poison into the skin that can create ongoing burning and even a festering wound. Its scientific name was well chosen: *Oplopanax horridus*.

Hikers and forest workers are well versed in its biting characteristic and it is often called the hiker's curse. Local people learn, the easy or hard way, how to recognize and avoid it. Devil's club grows in luxuriant, moist places, in swamps or along stream edges in a tangle of thorny stems and an explosion of leaves. A.O. Wheeler, an early 1900s topographer for the construction of the railways in the region, described it as "a bare stick an inch thick and five to eight feet high with a spread of tropical-looking palmated leaves at the top, set off by a bunch of bright red berries." A beauty indeed.

What I love so much about this plant is the phenomenal growth, symbol of its extreme success in its ecological niche. The leaves are huge. No dinner plates here but rather feast platters of an intense green. The shiny red pannicle of berries are glorious decoration for a splendid spread. And the stem is a vision of vigour, spreading as it does above and under the ground.

One day, my neighbour Jake handed me a small piece of wood, about a foot long and three or four centimetres in diameter. "What is it?" he asked, his eyes twinkling. Ah-ah! A trick. I hefted it my palm: it felt light. I pulled its smooth surface across my hand. I put it to my nose. And then there was no doubt.

"Devil's club," I told him. Delighted, but disappointed that he hadn't been able to trick me, he asked me how I knew. Nothing smells like devil's club does. Its strong, vaguely medicinal odour has the pungency of mushrooms but with the zing of green. As a member of the ginseng family it carries unique and potent substances within it.

I was not surprised to discover the serious medicinal properties of devil's club. The First Nations people have long used it to remedy various ailments. It is named in over 25 languages in North America and has had a high cultural importance as well as medicinal value. Its glycosides and aromatic oils affect the body's hypothalmic-pituitary axis. Its use as an herbal control for diabetes has been studied as well as its healing ability for rheumatoid arthritis and other autoimmune disorders. The Sinixt used it to treat consumption or a dry cough. Though it is a formidable plant in many ways, the medicine of the devil's club was known to be sensitive to disturbance. An infusion was placed by a creek to keep it cool, and one had to be careful not to allow the shadow of a person to pass over it. Modern herbalists echo the practices of ancient ones, in part, by recommending only a cold infusion of the roots. The uses of devil's club do not stop at the medicinal. The Sinixt apparently used the thorns for pinning and sewing together.

Thus, the spectacular xwuwwugwáy̓lhp, as it was known to the Sinixt, had a status far beyond that of its current notoriety as the bane of hikers. It was, and is, a reminder that what is fierce, formidable and even painful is to be honoured for the power it inevitably holds. So, do not tremble so much in fear as in deep respect when you step among its thorny glory but rather bow to its strength and beauty as you give it respectful berth. Long live devil's club!

Eileen

The highest reaches of the subalpine and alpine zones of our mountains are harsh and difficult places for vegetation. Trees are stunted by deep snowpack or scoured by icy winds. Flowering plants work within a tight timeline to bud, flower, fruit and flourish, all in the few months when no snow flies. My notebook records the texture of the high landscape: a sketch of Ymir Mountain (2,398 metres) with a few notes beside it. *Such downward vertical movement! Windswept — erosion-scarred — ravaged by the melt of snow.* I draw no flowers during that August hike, but instead list a handful of names of the blooms I see: Sitka valerian, alpine paintbrush, western pasque flower. The deep reds, purples and bright pinks do not, for some reason, find their way onto the page. Instead, one word describes the effect of the flowers spreading in densely populated meadows. *Triumph.* Colour sometimes pale by comparison to splendour. Despite the short growing season, the prolonged snow, and the harsh wind, delicate alpine flowers could thrive.

My favourite of all the alpine flowers is one that depends utterly on the wind to disperse its seed. The western pasque flower blooms early in the season, often before the snow is completely gone. I have never been high enough early enough to see it in bloom. But I know from my plant guidebook that it is, technically, a flower without any petals. Five or six curved white sepals surround the seed head to resemble petals. The mature plant, with its head of silky, disarrayed hair, is the stage of the flower I know best. Each strand of the hair on the seed head has a mature pod at its base, attached to the centre of what was once the bud. The individual tails on the pods crowd together on the flower's "scalp" to form a thick mop. I walk past the clusters of seed pod, watching the mop sway and dance with delightful freedom in the stiff wind. "My hair's a mess," the flower seems to be saying. "Ask me if I care."

Flowers in the anemone family are also called "windflowers", because the seeds need wind to spread. I like to imagine the silky, disarrayed pods being torn free at last by a harsh autumn wind that carries the first shreds of snow. In my mind's eye, I can see the pods floating across the tangle of other flowers touched by frost, searching for a new home before snow locks the alpine into frozen stillness.

I wish I could be as satisfied and self-reliant as a plant seems to be, blooming year after year, catching the wind, cradling rain, feeding the soil with its spent leaves.

K. Linda

The maidenhair fern that I find growing among the mossy abundance of Nemo Creek in Valhalla Provincial Park is the most beautiful of any fern I've encountered. Its tall glossy black stem is topped with a spray of leaves, like a hand with many delicate fingers. Growing near streams, these ferns greet passers-by, human, ungulate, rodent and ursine alike. Indigenous people of the Columbias have noted that where maidenhair fern grows, the grizzly is likely to walk as well.

I've often said, only somewhat in jest, that I'd like to come back in my next life — should there be one — as a fern. But as I've grown to know ferns, the issue has complicated itself. Which fern to return as? The common, rugged bracken, the edible fiddlehead of the ostrich fern, or something more delicate and unusual like maidenhair fern?

Even the thought of such a destiny sends a curious frisson of pleasure, not unlike the shiver of a fern, brushed past on a secretive forest path, down my spine. The fantasy of being something so ancient, so enduring, so flourishing, yet delicate pulls me out of the short sightedness of human time. Ferns, in spite of their gentle demeanour, have had a fierce hold on the Earth for a long, long time. They are older than all the flowering plants that evolved in tandem with the mammals and birds that relied on them. Their reproductive spores rained down on the dinosaurs, who stomped among their persistent growth.

How would it be to greet the other forest dwellers as a fern? They would not fear me, or I, them. To live a simple yet persistent life, as part of the Earth's gift of green. What more could I aspire to?

Acknowledgements

K. Linda

The Inner Green is the product of many years of interactions and conversations with people who share my love for this place we call home.

I've had the good fortune of sharing my home with my land partners, Joe Hetherington, Christopher Moore, Karen Newmoon, Jessica Manley and Martin Carver. They have been important companions in my explorations along with our wonderful neighbour, Jake Urech. To Luanne Armstrong, I am thankful for her passion for the land, her support of me as a writer, her friendship, and for moving this book along its path. Karen Warkentin continues to be a wonderful friend and a longstanding mentor in my discovery of the natural world. Long ago she planted a seed in me that grew into new eyes — I'm not sure where I'd be without the blessing of her influence in my life. I am grateful to my parents, Arnold and Niina Kivi, for teaching me where I come from and for their support in where I've chosen to go in my life.

I am grateful to many people for their assistance on specific chapters and issues: Carol Wallace, Lesley Anderton, Stan Rowe, Erica Mallam, Harry Quesnel, Marc-Andre Beaucher, Penny Ohanjanian, Greg Utzig, Don Gayton, Ted Antifeau, Michael Keefer and the Ktunaxa Elders Working Group. I also offer thanks to the Columbia Basin Trust for supporting this project with financial assistance.

My partner, Martin Carver, has given me immeasurable gifts. He incited me to write this book and nurtured my confidence throughout the project. I thank him for the time, care, concise thinking and adventurous spirit that contributed to the making of this book and our hand-crafted lives.

The Inner Green

Finally, I'd like to acknowledge a deep appreciation for my co-writer Eileen Delehanty Pearkes. I thank her for rising to the occasion, for meeting me on the path, for journeying together for awhile. Her awe, her passion, her curiosity, her struggles and her commitment are all an inspiration to me.

Eileen

Thank you to Timothy, George and Jack, for coming along on many journeys, and for being so patient with my curiosity. Amber and Lucy also helped out whenever they could.

When she invited me to join her project, K.Linda Kivi demonstrated a rare trait in writers: a willingness to share space on the title page. I admire her openess to artistic collaboration, as well as her keen perception and her determination.

Thank you to Greg Utzig and Joan Snyder who read early drafts and to Janice Logan for helping us trim branches. Charles Syrett, the amazing map guy, was generous with time and expertise.

Members of the Sinixt Nation have been generous with their knowledge and support of my learning. Randy Bouchard and Dorothy Kennedy carefully recorded many cultural practices, stories and place names of the Sinixt People before this information was lost.

The Nelson Museum, the Nelson Public Library, and the remarkable Kootenaiana Collection at the Selkirk College library are filled with treasures. Thank you Shawn Lamb, Deb Thomas, Liz Ball and staffs, for keeping watch. Alan Ramsden is a one-man miracle storehouse of landscape history. The Columbia Mountains Institute of Applied Ecology has provided many useful contacts and given me a forum to experience the "science side" of the landscape.

References

Epigraph
Oliver, Mary, *White Pine*, New York: Harcourt Brace & Co., 1994

The Weight of a Name
Epigraph: LeGuin, Ursula K. *Wild Oats and Fireweed*, New York. Harper and Row, 1988.
Anderton, Lesley, in conversation with, Castlegar, B.C., 2000.
Cannings, Sydney and Richard, *Geology of B.C.: A Journey Through Time*. Vancouver: Greystone Books, 1999.
Little, H.W. *Nelson Map-Area, West Half, B.C. Memoir 308*. Geological Survey of Canada, 1960.
McDonald, J.D. *The Story in the Rocks: The Geology of Rossland, B.C.* Rossland: Rossland Historical Museum Association, 1995.
Pielou, E.C. *After the Ice Age*. Chicago: University of Chicago Press, 1991.
Rice, H. *Nelson Map-Area East. Memoir 228*. Geological Survey of Canada, 1941.
Rowe, Stan, in conversation with, New Denver, B.C., 2001.
Yorath, C.J. *Where Terranes Collide*. Victoria: Orca Books, 1990, p. 110.

Going Squirrely:
Burton, Rebecca. "Attributes of Red Squirrel Caches in a Non-Serotinous Conifer Forest," *Northwestern Naturalist*, 79:108-112, 1998.
Hebers, Jim. Masters' thesis talk on "Red Squirrel Demography and Behaviour in a Managed Douglas-Fir Forest," for the Dead Ecologists Society, Nelson, August 2001.
Vander Wall, Stephen B. *Food Hoarding in Animals*. Chicago: University of Chicago Press, 1990, p. 68.

The Snow, The Snow
Formosov, A.N. *Snow Cover as an Integral Factor of the Environment and Its Importance in the Ecology of Mammals and Birds*. Edmonton: Boreal Institute for Northern Studies, 1964.
Kirk, Ruth. *Snow*. New York: William Morrow and Company, 1978.
Marchand, Peter. *Life in the Cold: An Introduction to Winter Ecology*. Hanover: University of New England, 1987.

Slow to Perfection
Blatt, Suzie E. and John H. Bordon. "Evidence for a male-produced aggregation pheromone in the Western conifer Seed Gub, Leptoglossus occidentalis Heidemann," *The Canadian Entomologist*. 128: 77-778, 1996.

The Inner Green

Fleischner, Thomas Lowe. *Singing Stone: A Natural History of the Escalante Canyons*. Salt Lake City: University of Utah Press, 1999, p. 40.

Furniss, R.L. and V.M. Carolin. *Western Forest Insects*. U.S. Forest Service Miscellaneous Publication 1339, 1977.

Ridge-O'Connor, Gale E. *The Western Conifer Seed Bug, Letoglossus occidentalis Heidemann*. Masters' Thesis, Southern Conneticut State University, 1998.

Waldbauer, Gilbert, *Insects through the Seasons*. Cambridge: Harvard University Press, 1996.

The Hieroglyphics of Extinction

Berry, Wendell. *Life is a Miracle*, Washington, D.C.: Counterpoint, 2000.

Bouchard, Randy and Dorothy Kennedy. *First Nations Ethnography and Ethnohistory in B.C.'s Lower Kootenay-Columbia Hydropower Region*. Castlegar, B.C: Columbia Power Corp., August, 2000.

Snyder, Joan, "Survival on the Hoof: Is Time Running Out for B.C.'s Mountain Caribou?" *B.C. Naturalist*. Winter, 2004.

Spry, Irene, ed. *The Papers of the Palliser Expedition, 1857-1860*. Toronto: The Champlain Society, 1968.

Thompson, David. *Journal Kept by David Thompson During His Travels in North America*. New York: Antiquarian Press Ltd., 1959.

Utzig, Greg, in conversation with, February, 2001.

The Tree Inside Me

Epigraph: a translation of Rainer Maria Rilke's poem found in Gaston Bachelard's *Poetics of Space*. Boston: Beacon Press, 1969.

Chadwick, Douglas H. "Nerd Science and Miracles in Subtropical Montana," from *The Roadless Yaak*, ed., Rick Bass, Conneticut: The Lyons Press, 2002.

Edmunds, Jain Claire Dirks. *Not Just Trees: The Legacy of a Douglas Fir Forest*." Pullman: Washington State University Press, 1999.

Peattie, D.C. *A Natural History of Western Trees*. Boston: Houghton-Mifflin, 1953.

Snake Day Tribute

St. Clair, Robert, "Identifying Critical Habitats for a Vulnerable Snake Species, The Rubber Boa." Columbia Basin Fish and Wildlife Compensation Program, 1999.

A Rare Night

Ohanjanian, Penny. *Report on the Coeur d'Alene Salamander (Plethodon idahoensis)*. B.C. Ministry of Forests, 1998.

Phillips, Kathryn. *Tracking the Vanishing Frogs*. New York: St. Martin's Press, 1994.

Ground Truth

Epigraph from LaChapelle, Dolores. *Sacred Land, Sacred Sex, Rapture of the Deep: concerning deep ecology and celebrating life.* Silverton, Colorado: U.S. Finn Hill Arts, c. 1988.

Baker, Rick and Martin Carver, in conversations with, Nelson, B.C., 1999.

Singing One's Heart Out

Armstrong, E.A. "Behavioural Adaptations of the Wren." *Biological Review.* 52:235-294, 1977.

Bagemihl, Bruce. *Biological Exuberance: Animal Homosexuality and Natural Diversity.* New York: St. Martin's Press, 1999.

Kroodsma, Donald E. "Winter Wren Singing Behaviour: A Pinnacle of Song Complexity," *The Condor,* 82:357-65, 1980.

Rowe, Stan. *Homeplace: Essays on Ecology.* Edmonton: NewWest Press, 2002.

Van Horne, Beatrice. "Assessing Vocal Variety in the Winter Wren, A Bird with a Complex Repertoire." *The Condor,* 97:39-49, 1995.

Wilcy, R. Haven. "A New Sense of the Complexities of Bird Song," *Auk.* 117:4, 2000.

Fish Out of Water

Bouchard, Randy and Dorothy Kennedy. *First Nations Ethnography and Ethnohistory in B.C.'s Lower Kootenay-Columbia Hydropower Region.* Castlegar, B.C: Columbia Power Corp., August, 2000.

Cole, Jean Murray, ed. *This Blessed Wilderness: Archibald MacDonald's Letters from the Columbia, 1832-44.* Vancouver, UBC Press, 2001.

Dove, Mourning. *Coyote Stories.* Lincoln: University of Nebraska Press, 2001.

Kennedy, Dorothy and Randy Bouchard. *Utilization of Fish by the Colville Okanagan Indian People.* Unpublished draft report, June 1975, courtesy of the authors.

Illuminating the Unseen

Clark, Ross. *South Selkirk Cougar Ecology and Predation Project: 1998-2001 Progress Report.* Columbia Basin Fish and Wildlife Compensation Program, 2001.

Hansen, Kevin. *Cougar: The American Lion.* Sacramento: Northland Publishing, 1992.

Milstein, Michael. "The Quiet Kill," *National Parks,* May/June, 1989.

Seidensticker, John C., M. Hornocker, W. Wiles and J. Messick. *Mountain Lion Social Organization in the Idaho Primitive Area.* Wildlife Monographs, 1974.

Awakening

Hinchman, Hannah. *A Trail Through the Leaves: the journal as a path to place.* New York: W.W. Norton, 1997.

Rowe, Stan J. and Erica Mallam. *The Gnome Plant.* Nelson: B.C. Parkes Kootenay District, 2000.

The Inner Green

General References

Abram, David. *The Spell of the Sensuous*. New York: Random House, 1996

Bass, Rick. The Roadless Yaak. Connecticut: Lyons Press, 2002.

Cannings, Sydney, Cannings, Richard, *British Columbia: A Natural History*. Vancouver, Greystone Books, 1996.

Careless, Ric. *To Save the Wild Earth*. Vancouver: Raincoast Books, 1997.

De Villiers, Marq. *Water*. Toronto: Stoddart, 2000.

Fleischner, Thomas Lowe. *Singing Stone: A Natural History of the Escalante Canyons*. Salt Lake City: University of Utah Press, 1999.

Gadd, Ben. *Handbook of the Canadian Rockies*. Jasper: Corax Press, 1986

Glavin, Terry. *The Last Great Sea: A voyage through the human and natural history of the North Pacific ocean*. Vancouver: Douglas and McIntyre, 2000.

Macy, Joanna and Molly Young Brown. *Coming Back to Life: Practices to Reconnect Our Lives, Our World*. Gabriola Island: New Society Publishers, 1998.

Nagorsen, David, W., Brigham, R.Mark., *Bats of British Columbia*. Vancouver: UB.C. Press, 1993.

Nisbet, Jack. *Sources of the River*. Seattle: Sasquatch Books, 1994.

Parish, Roberta, Ray Coupe, Dennis Lloyd, eds. *Plants of Southern Interior British Columbia*. Vancouver: Lone Pine Publishing, 1996.

Pearkes, Eileen Delehanty. *The Geography of Memory*. Kutenai House Press, 2002.

Pielou, E.C., *The World of Northern Evergreens*. Ithaca: Comstock Publishing Associates, 1988.

Pielou, E.C. *Fresh Water*. Chicago: University of Chicago Press, 1998.

Price, Paula. *Keeping the Lakes Way*. Toronto: University of Toronto Press, 1999.

Rowe, Stan. Homeplace: *Essays on Ecology*. Edmonton: NewWest Press, 2002.

Snyder, Gary. *A Place in Space*. Washington, D.C.: Counterpoint.1995.

Turner, Nancy J. *Food Plants of Interior First Peoples*. Vancouver: UBC Press, 1997.

Utzig, Greg, et. All. "Descriptions of the Central and Southern Columbia Mountain Ecosections," B.C. Parks, 2003.

Selected Animals and Plants of the Columbia Mountains

R= red-listed (endangered)   B= blue-listed (threatened)   E= extirpated

Common Name	Scientific name	Status

Insects:

Cedar bug/Western conifer seed bug	*Leptoglossus occidentalis*	
Snow cranefly	*Chionea spp*	
Water striders	*Gerridae family*	

Reptiles and Amphibians:

Long-toed salamander	*Ambystoma macrodactylum*	
Coeur d'Alene salamander	*Plethodon idahoensis*	B
Northern leopard frog	*Rana pipiens*	R
Western terrestrial garter snake	*Thamnophis elegans*	
Common garter snake	*Thamnophis sirtalis*	
Rubber boa	*Charina bottae*	B

Fish:

Mottled sculpin	*Cottus bairdi*	B
Shorthead sculpin	*Cottus confusus*	B
White sturgeon	*Acipenser transmontanus*	R
Bull trout	*Salvelinus confluentus*	B
Rainbow trout	*Oncorhynchus mykiss*	
Brook trout	*Salvelinus fontinalis*	
Burbot	*Lota iota*	

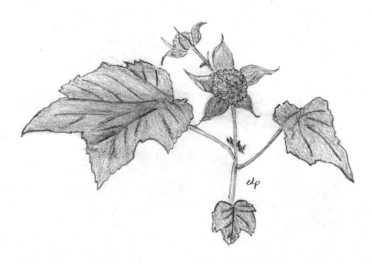

Umatilla dace	*Rhinichthys umatilla*	R
Kokanee	*Oncorhynchus nerka*	
Coho salmon	*Oncorhynchus kisutch*	E
Chinook (spring) salmon	*Oncorhynchus gorbuscha*	E
Sockeye salmon	*Oncorhynchus nerka*	E

Birds:

Western grebe	*Aechmophorus occidentalis*	R
Great blue heron	*Ardea herodius*	B
Canada goose	*Branta canadensis*	
Harlequin duck	*Histrionicus histrionicus*	
Common merganser	*Mergus merganser*	
Osprey	*Pandion haliaetus*	
Bald eagle	*Haliaeetus leucocephalus*	
White-tailed ptarmigan	*Lagopus leucurus*	
Ruffed grouse	*Bonasa umbellus*	
Wild turkey	*Meleagris gallopavo*	
Western screech owl	*Otus kennicottii*	R
Great horned owl	*Bub virginianus*	
Northern hawk owl	*Surnia ulula*	
Northern pygmy owl	*Glaucidium gnoma*	
Barred owl	*Strix varia*	
Great Gray owl	*Strix nebulosa*	
Long-eared owl	*Asio otus*	
Short-eared owl	*Asio flammeus*	B
Boreal owl	*Aegolius funereus*	
Northern saw-whet owl	*Aegolius acadicus*	
Rufus hummingbird	*Selasphorus rufus*	
Belted kingfisher	*Ceryle alcyon*	
Downy woodpecker	*Picoides pubescens*	
Hairy woodpecker	*Picoides villosus*	
Northern flicker	*Colaptes auratus*	

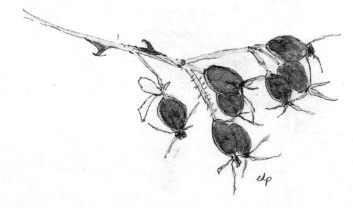

edp

Pileated woodpecker	*Dryocopus pileatus*
Stellar's jay	*Cyanocitta stelleri*
Clark's nutcracker	*Nucifraga columbiana*
American crow	*Corvus brachyrhynchos*
Common raven	*Corvus corax*
Black-capped chickadee	*Parus atricapillus*
Red-breasted nuthatch	*Sitta canadensis*
White-breasted nuthatch	*Sitta carolinensis*
Winter wren	*Troglodytes troglodytes*
American dipper	*Cinclus mexicanus*
Golden-crowned kinglet	*Regulus satrapa*
Ruby-crowned kinglet	*Regulus calendula*
Varied thrush	*Ixoreus naevius*
Dark-eyed junco	*Junco hyemalis*
Pine siskin	*Caruelis pinus*

Mammals:

Pika	*Ochotona princeps*	
Snowshoe hare	*Lepus americanus*	
Meadow vole	*Microtus pennsylvanicus*	
Heather vole	*Phenacomys intermedius*	
Long-tailed vole	*Microtus longicaudus*	
Bushy-tailed woodrat (aka packrat)	*Neotoma cinerea*	
Deer mouse	*Peromyscus municulatus*	
Porcupine	*Erethizon dorsatum*	
Northern flying squirrel	*Glaucomys sabrinus*	
Columbia ground squirrel	*Spermophilus columbianus*	
Yellow-pine chipmunk	*Eutamias amoenus*	
Red squirrel	*Tamiasciurus hudsonicus*	
Coyote	*Canis latrans*	
Grey wolf	*Canis lupus*	
Cougar	*Puma concolor*	
Lynx	*Felis lynx*	
Wolverine	*Gulo gulo luscus*	B
Marten	*Martes americana*	
Long-tailed weasel	*Mustela nivalis*	
Black bear	*Ursus americanus*	
Grizzly bear	*Ursus arctos*	B
Moose	*Alces alces*	
Rocky Mountain elk	*Cervus elaphus*	
Mule deer	*Odocoileus hemionus*	
White-tailed deer	*Odocoileus virginianus*	
Mountain goat	*Oreamnos americanus*	
Caribou	*Rangifer tarandus*	R

Plants:

Alder, sitka	*Alnus, cripsa*
Aspen, trembling	*Populus tremuloides*
Aster, leafy	*Aster foliaceus*
Bastard toad-flax	*Geocaulon lividum*
Bear-grass	*Xerophyllum tenax*
Birch, paper	*Betula papyrifera*
Bitterroot	*Lewisia rediviva*
Black sanicle	*Sanicula marilandica*
Burdock, great	*Arctium lappa*
Camas, death	*Zigadenus venernosus*
Cedar, western red	*Thuja plicata*
Cottonwood, black	*Populus balsamifera spp. trichocarpa*
Cow-parsnip	*Heracleum lanatum*
Devil's club	*Oplopanax horridus*
Dogbane, hemp	*Apocynum cannabinum*
Dogwood, red-osier	*Cornus stolonifera*
Douglas-fir	*Pseudotsuga menziesii*
Elderberry, blue	*Sambucus caerulea*
False solomon's seal	*Smilacina racemosa*
Falsebox	*Pachistima myrsinites*
Fern, maidenhair	*Adiantum pedatum*
ostrich	*Matteucia struthiopteris*
bracken	*Pteridium aquilinum*
western licorice	*Polypodium hesperium*
Fir, subalpine	*Abies lasiocarpa*
Fireweed	*Epilobium augustifolia*
Ginger, wild	*Asarum caudatum*
Gnome plant	*Hemitomes congestum*
Heather, pink	*Phyllodoce empetriformis*
white	*Cassiope mertensiana*
Hellebore, Indian	*Veratrum viride*
Hemlock, western	*Tsuga heterophylla*
Hemp dogbane	*Apocynum cannabinum*
Horsetail, common	*Equisetum arvense*
Hound's-tongue, common	*Cynoglossum officinale*
Huckleberry, black	*Vaccinium membranaceum*
Larch, western	*Larix occidentalis*
Lichens, frecklepelt	*Peltigera aphthosa*
Common witch's hair	*Alectoria sarmentosa*
Horsehairs	*Bryoria, sp.*
Monk's-hood	*Hypogymnia sp.*
Lime dust	*Chrysothrix chlorina*
Locoweed	*Oxytropis campestris*
Maple, douglas	*Acer glabrum*

Monkey-flower, pink	*Mimulus lewisii*
Moss, step	*Hylocomium splendens*
Mountain ash, western	*Sorbus scopulina*
Nightshade, enchanter's	*Circaea alpina*
Oregon grape	*Mahonia aquifolium*
Paintbrush, alpine	*Castilleja rhexifolia*
Pasqueflower, western	*Anemone occidentalis*
Pine western white	*Pinus monticola*
ponderosa	*Pinus ponderosa*
lodgepole	*Pinus contorta*
Prince's pipe	*Chimaphila umbellata*
Queen's cup	*Clintonia uniflora*
Rose, prickly	*Rosa acicularis*
Sage	*Artemisia tridentate*
Salal	*Gaultheria shallon*
Sarsaparilla	*Aralia mudicaulis*
Saskatoon	*Amelanchier alnifolia*
Saxifrage, spotted	*Saxifaga bronchialis*
Self-heal	*Prunella vulgaris*
Shepherd's purse	*Capsella bursa-pastoris*
Skunk cabbage	*Lysichiton americanum*
Snowberry	*Symphoricarpos albus*
Soopolallie	*Shepherdia canadensis*
Spring beauty	*Claytonia laneolata*
Spruce, englemann	*Picea engelmannii*
Sundew, round-leafed	*Drosera rotundifolia*
Thimbleberry	*Rubus parviflorus*
Twisted stalk	*Streptopus amplexifolius*
Valerian, sitka	*Valeriana sitchensis*
Western pasqueflower	*Anemone occidentalis*
Western tea-Berry	*Gaultheria ovatifolia*
Willow (scrub)	*Salix, spp.*